Pentecostal Theology

and the Christian

Spiritual Tradition

Simon Chan

WIPF & STOCK · Eugene, Oregon

For my wife

Wipf and Stock Publishers
199 W 8th Ave, Suite 3
Eugene, OR 97401

Pentecostal Theology and the Christian Spiritual Tradition
By Chan, Simon
Copyright©2000 by Chan, Simon
ISBN 13: 978-1-61097-084-6
Publication date 5/1/2011
Previously published by Sheffield Academic Press, 2000

CONTENTS

INTRODUCTION

This study seeks to interpret the Pentecostal reality in the light of the Christian spiritual tradition, and in so doing, address the problem of Pentecostal traditioning. By Pentecostal reality, I am referring to a cluster of experiences which, Pentecostals believe, distinguish them from other Christians. Pentecostals themselves are not in agreement over the precise nature of their distinctives. But what comes through over and over again in their discussions and writings is a certain kind of spiritual experience of an intense, direct and overwhelming nature centring in the person of Christ which they schematize as 'baptism in the Holy Spirit'.[1] For too long Pentecostals have been trying to defend their Pentecostal distinctiveness, but often at the expense of cutting themselves from the mainstream of Christian tradition. They are afraid that by identifying too closely with the mainstream they might lose their distinctiveness. I would like to argue, on the contrary, that it is when Pentecostals come to see their distinctives as a part of the larger tradition that they can preserve them and maintain their integrity. Pentecostals, as a matter of fact, could not avoid forging links with other Christian bodies; the problem is who they link up with.

Walter Hollenweger has maintained that the heart or core of the Pentecostal reality is found in the first five or ten years of the movement.[2] With this assessment Steven Land agrees and has attempted to capture this 'core' in his book *Pentecostal Spirituality: A Passion for the Kingdom*.[3] One does see something of the wholesomeness and beauty in Land's portrayal of Pentecostal spirituality, even if some of it seems to represent an 'ideal-type' construction rather than historical description. A character like William J. Seymour (1870–1922) comes close to em-

1. Mathew S. Clark *et al.*, *What is Distinctive About Pentecostal Theology?* (Pretoria: University of South Africa, 1989), pp. 163-69.

2. W. Hollenweger, 'Pentecostals and the Charismatic Movement', in C. Jones, G. Wainwright and S.J. Edward Yarnold (eds.), *The Study of Spirituality* (London: SPCK, 1986), pp. 549-54 (551).

3. Sheffield: Sheffield Academic Press, 1993.

bodying the Pentecostal ideal type.[4] But if Hollenweger's observation is right, it raises an alarming question: Why did Pentecostalism so quickly depart from its core and evolve into a segregationist, individualistic, culture-bound and inward-looking faith?

There is no question that classical Pentecostalism after almost a century is experiencing spiritual fatigue. Signs are everywhere of the waning of zeal and missionary vision. From published reports AG churches in USA are not growing. In one particular year the entire AG denomination in the USA experienced a net growth of one church.[5] Del Tarr stated that in 'hundreds of USA churches...there is no growth because there is no witness'—and he was being 'conservative' in his estimate of the numbers.[6] The social researches of Margaret Poloma indicate that the denomination is undergoing a phase of development which Max Weber called the 'routinization of charisma'. Even though glossolalia is a central doctrine, statistics show that a sizeable number of AG adherents do not speak in tongues or have stopped doing so.[7]

Signs of panic are also apparent. On the one hand, the 'establishment' Pentecostals appear more and more to align themselves with the fundamentalists. Attempts at reintroducing the King James Bible and censuring ministers involved in ecumenical dialogue are perhaps indicative of a leadership that feels that it is slowly losing its grip.[8] Hard-core dogmatism is always self-reassuring! On the other hand, those who are feeling the 'routinization of charisma' are searching desperately for new experiences. Where do they turn but to places where a lot of action seems to be going on: Toronto, Pensacola and a host of independent charismatic churches? But what the seekers are offered there are mostly exciting experiences whose novelty quickly wears off and which have

4.   See Douglas J. Nelson, 'For Such a Time as This: The Story of Bishop William J. Seymour and the Azusa Street Mission' (PhD dissertation, University of Birmingham, 1981).

5.   'U.S. A/G Churches Opened and Closed: 1965–1998'. Office of General Secretary, General Council of the Assemblies of God. The information was supplied by Cecil M. Robeck, Jr, in conversation.

6.   'Transcendence and Immanence and the Emerging Pentecostal Academy', in Robert Menzies and Wonsuk Ma (eds.), *Pentecostalism in Context* (Sheffield: Sheffield Academic Press, 1997), pp. 195-222.

7.   Margaret Poloma, *The Assemblies of God at the Crossroads: Charisma and Institutional Dilemmas* (Knoxville, TN: University of Tennessee Press, 1988), p. 40.

8.   These were some of the resolutions brought to the general council of the Assemblies of God of USA in recent years.

to be replaced by new experiences. We have here a religious version of the fashion world. The typical Pentecostal-charismatic church today is far from being a 'contrast community'; it is in fact the epitome of modern culture.

But Pentecostalism, as Hollenweger has also pointed out, has a tradition of self-criticism.[9] Throughout its history there have been prophetic voices castigating abuses of spiritual power and alerting the movement to the danger of compromise with the world. We think of Frank Bartleman, an early Pentecostal who was a witness of the Azusa Street revival, and more recently David Wilkerson and a growing number of veritable Pentecostals (and scholars) who are trying to set their own house in order. Bartleman has this to say of his age:

> We live in a light jazzy age... They refuse the fires of purifying, holiness of heart. We have an atmosphere of confusion. There is too much 'professional' work, railroading seekers through, like a 'quack' doctor's office. This produces a 'fake' Pentecost, with spurious 'tongues'. The 'singing in the Spirit' is also imitated. Men have learned to do these things without the Spirit, and suggest them to others for their imitation. We have even heard leaders call for any demonstration they wanted from the people. What would Peter say to such a demonstration?... We advertise 'miracles', wonderful preachers, etc., and have crowds following bill-board 'signs' to the next big meeting.[10]

We are seeing something very similar today. Spiritual power is being manipulated by charismatic gnostics and magicians who seem to have access to privileged information about principalities and powers and how to outmanoeuvre them. Instead of serious discipleship we have virtual fan clubs revolving around the mega-church leader. Seldom is worship an encounter with the awesome God; it has become an occasion for cheap thrills and continuous festivity dubiously called 'praise and worship'. Pentecostal scholars today are seriously addressing these issues in line with their critical tradition, as can be seen in a sizeable number of articles in journals like *Pneuma*.[11] Sadly, it is the Pentecostal denominational headquarters that are reticent about the problem, being more concerned with the status quo.[12]

---

9. Walter Hollenweger, 'The Critical Tradition of Pentecostalism', *Journal of Pentacostal Theology* 1 (1992), pp. 7-17.

10. Cited by Land, *Pentecostal Spirituality*, p. 51.

11. See, e.g., *Pneuma* 13.1 (1991).

12. Hollenweger, 'The Critical Tradition', p. 14.

The problem has a number of causes, but the main one is the failure in traditioning. The Pentecostal reality has not been communicated in all its fullness to a subsequent generation. When it was explained, it came through as rather impoverished theological constructs. To cite a case in point, the central doctrine called 'baptism in the Spirit' is far richer in Pentecostal *experience* than in Pentecostal *explanation*. As experience, it is nothing less than the 'revelation' of the triune God,[13] a 'theophany' of the God of history and the eschaton;[14] yet when it was explained, it was narrowly defined as 'the enduement of power for life and service'. This disparity between experience and explanation has serious consequences for Pentecostal traditioning. We could better clarify the nature of the problem by looking at it in the light of George Lindbeck's 'cultural linguistic' theory of doctrine.[15] According to Lindbeck, doctrines are like the regulative grammar that a community devises in order to make sense of their particular way of life. So, when Pentecostals explain glossolalia as the initial physical evidence of Spirit-baptism, *within* the Pentecostal community, as Joel Shuman has shown in a recent article,[16] this makes pretty good sense. But it makes good sense only as long as the majority of the people in the community continue to have a healthy experience of the Pentecostal reality—which was not a problem in the early days when most Pentecostals experienced Spirit-baptism and glossolalia first hand. But when the experience is inadequately conceptualized, what is communicated to the next generation is a constricted concept of the experience, and this concept will in turn evoke an equally narrow experience. This, I believe, is what is happening to Pentecostal believers in our churches today. Among second-generation Pentecostals Spirit-baptism is received first as a doctrine before it is actualized in personal experience. But when the doctrine is poorly explained, the intended experience does not necessarily follow. Or, one may have had an experience of glossolalia, but over time when questions begin to arise concerning the adequacy of the

13. Peter Hocken, 'The Meaning and Purpose of "Baptism in the Spirit" ', *Pneuma* 7.2 (Fall 1985), pp. 125-34 (125).

14. Frank D. Macchia, 'Sighs Too Deep For Words: Toward a Theology of Glossolalia', *Journal of Pentecostal Theology* 1 (1992), pp. 47-73 (55-60).

15. George A. Lindbeck, *The Nature of Doctrine: Religion and Theology in a Postliberal Age* (Philadelphia: Westminster Press, 1984).

16. Joel Shuman, 'Toward A Cultural-Linguistic Account of the Pentecostal Doctrine of the Baptism of the Holy Spirit', *Pneuma* 19.2 (Fall 1997), pp. 207-23.

traditional Pentecostal explanation, one begins to cast doubt on one's own experience. If Pentecostals hope to communicate the original reality to subsequent generations, they must come up with an explanation that encapsulates it adequately.

But this failure in traditioning is symptomatic of a larger problem, namely, the lack of awareness of being a part of the larger Christian tradition. Lacking that awareness, Pentecostalism is not able to harness the conceptual tools the Christian tradition provides which would have enabled it to interpret its own experience more adequately. Here, Pentecostals are caught in a dilemma. On the one hand, they want to maintain their distinctive experience and this often means having to define it against the mainstream interpretation. Yet, on the other hand, they feel the need to establish their orthodox credentials by identifying themselves with some larger Christian body. Pentecostals, unfortunately, had not been very judicious in their choice of allies in the past. As Gerald Sheppard has noted, the questionable alliance that Pentecostalism made with dispensationalism only succeeded in undermining its own theological integrity.[17] Yet, as Pentecostals sought to clarify their own identity at the beginning of the twenty-first century, they have also found their affinities with other traditions besides the evangelicals, like the Pietistic stream that flows within the more liberal wing of Protestantism.[18] This is a good start, but what Pentecostals need is to discover the deeper roots of their faith and experience. There is much in the contemplative tradition which resonates with Pentecostalism which Pentecostals need to explore further. Catholic charismatics have been quick to root their newly discovered experience in their own spiritual tradition. This has resulted in a much more coherent understanding of the key Pentecostal experiences of Spirit-baptism and glossolalia compared with the classical Pentecostal's own understanding. Their explanation and approach to these realities are generally more congenial towards the Pentecostal self-understanding than those provided by most evangelicals, even by those evangelicals who claim to be practitioners of glossolalia.[19]

17. Gerald Sheppard, 'Pentecostalism and the Hermeneutics and Dispensationalism: The Anatomy of an Uneasy Relationship', *Pneuma* 6.2 (Fall 1984), pp. 5-34.

18. See D. William Faupel, 'Whither Pentecostalism?' *Pneuma* 15.1 (Spring 1993), pp. 9-27.

19. Max Turner is one such evangelical. While sympathetic to tongues per se, his approach to the place of tongues in relation to Spirit-baptism will in the end leave less room for Pentecostals to develop their own self-understanding with

The tension between continuity and discontinuity with the larger Christian tradition is something Pentecostals continue to struggle with. That there is something distinctive in Pentecostal experience is a point that recent Pentecostal scholars like Robert Menzies, Roger Stronstad and Steven Land have argued with a high level of sophistication. But how is this discontinuity to be maintained along with Pentecostal continuity with the larger Christian tradition? This question needs to be addressed if Pentecostals are to maintain their distinctiveness without marginalizing themselves.

If Pentecostals today are to recover the full-orbed Pentecostal reality of the first ten years, they will need to enlarge their understanding of key concepts like Spirit-baptism and glossolalia. They must not stop at chronicling their own history, writing commentaries and doing biblical theology, though these are very important in themselves. They must engage in integrative thinking, in systematic theology. Lukan pneumatology will have to be integrated with Pauline pneumatology and this integrated pneumatology will have to be interpreted within the larger framework of trinitarian theology. The failure in traditioning could also be seen as a failure in systematic theology. But Pentecostals need to go beyond having just the right theological concepts. Pentecostals are, quite understandably, afraid that the 'letter' might kill the 'spirit'. But they need not fear if they understand that this dualism between letter and spirit is itself a product of a certain kind of modern epistemology, namely, the Cartesian dualistic epistemology. What they need is to recover the ancient art of spiritual theology where reflecting on the nature of God and praying to him are indistinguishable acts. Only a spiritual theology will save Pentecostals from the trap of mere intellectualization of the faith.

In order to ground the Pentecostal reality in the larger Christian spiritual tradition, I would like to focus on two key concepts: glossolalia and baptism in the Spirit. But why glossolalia and baptism in the Spirit in particular? One could, ostensibly, consider a number of other Pentecostal practices in the light of the Christian tradition and derive much benefit from the comparison. The Pentecostal-charismatic penchant for dreams and visions, for instance, could be fruitfully explored in the light of similar phenomena in late medieval mysticism. In this endeavour, we would have the advantage of the monumental work of Bernard

respect to tongues compared with, say, the approach of Catholic Simon Tugwell. See Chapter 2.

McGinn.[20] But glossolalia and what it is believed to signify, baptism in the Spirit, are the most significant symbols of the Pentecostal movement. They are recognized in Pentecostal circles as the movement's most distinguishing marks. These terms, therefore, provide the means to explore meaningfully the distinctive features of Pentecostal experience. I would like to show that glossolalia which Pentecostals identify as 'the initial evidence' of baptism in the Spirit is a rich theological symbol precisely because it is linked to a reality (Spirit-baptism) which is far bigger than the classical Pentecostal conceptualization of it. Pentecostals also recognize that glossolalia has more than evidential value. It is also prayer, and as prayer it covers a very significant part of the Christian life of prayer when it is understood within the larger Christian spiritual tradition. Here, I would like to argue that glossolalia symbolizes the ascetical dimension of the Christian life just as evidential tongues symbolize the passive dimension. Together, we have a rich symbol that could integrate the passive and active dimensions of Christian spirituality.

But the analysis of Pentecostal experience per se is not enough. If traditioning is to be effective, it has to be carried out in the ecclesial community.[21] The Pentecostal church must become the traditioning community for Pentecostal faith and practice. But here, the Pentecostal church faces two formidable challenges. First, Pentecostalism thus far has been too individualistic in its conception of the spiritual life. The church is usually seen as a 'fellowship' to meet 'my needs'. It needs to move to a more communal understanding of the Christian life. In fact, Pentecostalism's central experience, as we have already said, makes much better sense when interpreted within its own communal-liturgical context. The Pentecostal Christian needs a Pentecostal community to make sense of his or her own spiritual experience. The second chal-

20. Bernard McGinn, *The Presence of God: A History of Western Mysticism* (London: SCM Press, 1991–), a monumental five-volume work, three of which are published: *The Foundation of Mysticism* (1991), *The Growth of Mysticism* (1994) and *The Flowering of Mysticism* (1998).

21. The need for Pentecostal scholars to do their theology within the worshipping Pentecostal community was underscored by John Christopher Thomas in his presidential address to the Society for Pentecostal Studies (pp. 7-8) in 'Pentecostal Theology in the Twenty-First Century', *Pneuma* 20.1 (Spring 1998), pp. 3-19. Thomas goes on to propose an outline of a Pentecostal ecclesiology based on the five-fold gospel and, on the same basis, makes an interesting suggestion on 'reappropriating the sacraments' (pp. 17-19).

lenge we face is that we are living in times when the general drift of many ecclesiastical traditions is towards the 'free church', non-hierarchical type, as Miroslav Volf has pointed out recently in his important study on ecclesiology.[22] Even Roman Catholicism and Eastern Orthodoxy are not spared. One can understand why a movement that cherishes the freedom of the Spirit would find the free church type more congenial. But if the Pentecostal movement is to bequeath its heritage to the next generation without diluting the core, it needs to have an adequate traditioning structure. I'm not referring here to ecclesiastical structures, hierarchy and such like; rather, I am referring to the need to develop an ecclesiology which makes effective traditioning possible.

Historically, there are both hierarchical as well as 'democratic' Pentecostal churches. The former is perhaps best (or should we say, worst?) represented by the modern charismatic mega-church which is the almost perfect embodiment of the effective, smooth-running hierarchy. But we are not so much concerned with ecclesiastical structures as with the theological nature of the church. The issue is not whether the church should be structured democratically or hierarchically, but whether it is a faithful and effective bearer of the Christian tradition. For the Pentecostal church to become an effective bearer of its own tradition, there needs to be a radical re-visioning of the church. The church needs to be seen not primarily as a functional entity for the sake of organizing our work more efficiently but as supremely a spiritual reality which, though existing in space and time, transcends space and time. The church is not the sum-total of individual Christians but exists prior to the individuals. To understand the church in this way, we need to reconsider the place of the sacraments and pneumatology. Only a proper theology of the sacraments and pneumatology can overcome the tendency to turn church services into what Gordon Fee calls 'a thousand individual experiences of worship'.[23] Pentecostals need to see beyond a doctrine of the Spirit as 'my personal Comforter' to one that sees the Spirit as first and foremost the Spirit for the *church* coming from *beyond* history. The implications of this for the life of worship are indeed far-reaching. Here, Pentecostals can learn much from Eastern Orthodoxy.

22. Miroslav Volf, *After our Likeness: The Church as the Image of the Trinity* (Grand Rapids: Eerdmans, 1998), pp. 12-13.

23. Gordon Fee, *The First Epistle to the Corinthians* (Grand Rapids: Eerdmans, 1987), p. 667.

In this connection, it is heartening to note the formation of the Charismatic Episcopal Church in 1992 by some 'independent pentecostal-charismatic congregations'. What is most interesting about it is that it is seeking to 'combine the elements of charismatic ministry with sacramental worship and celebrate biblical values and orthodox, evangelical teaching'. It wants to recover the catholicity of the church by 'restoring the liturgy, sacraments, creeds and councils of the early church to their proper place in our doctrine and worship'. At the same time it wants to integrate it with the evangelical conviction of personal conversion and charismatic gifts.[24] What we see in the Charismatic Episcopal Church is that the Pentecostal reality need not be confined to one particular type of church structure. In fact, I would like to show that it is better traditioned in a church that recognizes the constitutive role of the sacraments and the Spirit.

A radical re-visioning of the church will also help Pentecostals to recover a sense of genuine solidarity with all Christians that goes beyond the warm affinities with fellow-charismatics and fellow-Evangelicals. This was the original impulse of early Pentecostalism. The Pentecostal ecclesial *experience* has been more broadly ecumenical than its ecclesiology. Pioneers like William Seymour achieved a remarkable integration between blacks and whites. Later, David du Plessis initiated dialogue with the WCC at a time when conservative Christians were still highly suspicious of mainline Protestantism. In its more recent history Pentecostals like Cecil M. Robeck, Jr. continue to engage actively in dialogue with other Christians including Roman Catholics and Orthodox Christians—much to the consternation of the Pentecostal 'establishment'.

Pentecostals need to re-vision the church as an eschatological community which includes an apocalyptic dimension but is not confined to it. William Faupel has shown the importance of eschatology for Pentecostal faith and practice.[25] But their historical association with dispensationalism has led most of them to develop a crisis eschatology. While this has positive results in terms of mission, it has also tended to create a loose ecclesial structure which prevents effective traditioning. If Jesus is coming 'at any moment', the only thing worth doing is to preach the

24. Information taken from the web page of the Charismatic Episcopal Church (http://www.iccec.org).

25. D. William Faupel, *The Everlasting Gospel* (Sheffield: Sheffield Academic Press, 1996).

gospel. Three or four years of Bible school might well be redundant. A proper understanding of the church as an eschatological community, on the other hand, makes it possible for a more structured community to emerge whether Free Church or Episcopal. What is important is for that community to see how the Spirit of the 'last days' who 'constituted' the church (Zizioulas) creates a distinct entity that influences the world by its own distinctive character (Hauerwas).

The substance of these four chapters was first put together for the 1999 Annual Lectureship of the Asia-Pacific Theological Seminary in Baguio City, Philippines. I would like to express my gratitude to the seminary community for their warm reception and hospitality. Special mention must be made of Prof. Wonsuk Ma who not only initiated the invitation but also subsequently sent me materials I needed for revising the lectures and bringing them to their present form. Chapter 1 incorporated materials from the Thirty-Fifth Annual Lecture given at Morling College, Sydney. Chapter 2 appeared in a slightly different form as 'Evidential Tongues and the Doctrine of Subsequence' in the July 1999 issue of *Asian Journal of Pentecostal Studies*. A shorter version of Chapter 4 formed part of a series of lectures given at the Burleigh Conference 1999 in Adelaide. I would like to thank the organizers of the Conference in the South Australia Baptist Union who had enough faith in a Pentecostal preacher to invite him to be the main conference speaker. It was the enthusiastic response of these Baptist pastors that gave me hope that the tentative ideas on ecclesiology could be fruitfully employed even in the Free Church tradition. The assistance of two of my colleagues at Trinity Theological College deserves special mention. Dr Daniel Koh read the final proofs at short notice and Ms Lau Jen Sin our indefatigable librarian helped secure most of the materials I needed. Two important books, however, came too late for inclusion in the discussion on ecclesiology, Douglas Farrow's *Ascension and Ecclesia* and Reinhard Hütter's *Suffering Divine Things*, both from Eerdmans. I have taken these into consideration in an article in the Fall 2000 issue of the journal *Pneuma*. The book is affectionately dedicated to my wife, Myrna, whose singular commitment to ministry over twenty-three years has made many undertakings possible, including the writing of this book. Deo Gloria!

Chapter 1

THE TRADITIONING PROCESS

The Nature of Traditioning

Tradition, far from confining a community to a static existence, is, as Hauerwas has pointed out, the bearer of real change.[1] A community that seeks consciously to preserve its own values and way of life is more likely to be open to change as it faces new challenges than one that has no *explicit* traditions. We are all creatures of habit, and the most binding habits are those that we hold unthinkingly and subconsciously. But when values are embodied in a clearly defined and coherently developed system of thought, we can become more self-critical. It is when ideas are not well reflected upon that they tend to play on our unconscious fear of losing them: we begin to hold on to them with blind tenacity. In short, hazy theology is the bearer of a dead traditionalism, while a clearly articulated theology makes possible a living tradition that is responsive to change.

Traditioning is by nature a communal affair. This does not mean that individuals are not involved or do not contribute significantly to the development of a tradition. What it does mean is that the individuals contribute to the community *as* a member of that community, never apart from it. Much of the work that eventually became a part of a community's tradition is done by the leaders, thinkers and poets of that community. In the case of the ecclesial community, it's the prophets, priests and theologians.[2] But what is the role of the ecclesiastical leaders? I think this question needs a minor digression in view of the popular misconception about the nature of church leadership. A popular

1. Stanley Hauerwas, *A Community of Character: Toward a Constructive Christian Social Ethic* (Notre Dame: University of Notre Dame Press, 1981), p. 26.

2. For the functions of the prophet, priest and theologian in a theological community, see Robert J. Schreiter, *Constructing Local Theologies* (London: SCM Press, 1985), pp. 16-20.

notion of leadership is that the leader is the man or woman 'with a vision' for the church. Leaders do the thinking while the rest of the community are simply passive followers. This view of leadership subverts the biblical concept of the church. All Christians would readily agree that the church is the body of Christ and that Christ is the only and true head of the church. But the crucial question is, how does Christ lead his church? One view is that Christ leads through a person or through a small group of leaders. Leaders function as mediators standing between God and his people. They mediate the will of Christ to the ordinary members of the church. This is usually what 'the-man-with-a-vision' type of leadership is understood to mean. The leader hears from God and communicates the divine will to the church. Such a view is no better than a Protestant version of mediaeval priestcraft. Another view takes the opposite stance. Since the church is the body of Christ, Christ communicates to the entire body. Therefore one is as good as the other in hearing from God and communicating God's will. This view is right in its belief but wrong in its conclusion. It often results in a purely egalitarian community in which everyone is potentially, if not actually, a mouthpiece of God. The result is contradiction, confusion and finally division. History has furnished us with many examples of such communities that survived through schisms because everyone is potentially, if not actually, a leader: if everyone is a leader then there is really no leadership. A proper view of the real role of prophets, priests and theologians must maintain both the integrity of Christ's headship of the church and the distinctiveness of ecclesiastical leaders. First, the leaders are able to help the community define itself and its role in the larger society only if they are sensitive to the tradition of the community. If they could feel the pulse of the community, they could lead the church forward to face new challenges. Second, their task is not to impose their own vision upon the church, but to make explicit what is implicit among the less articulate or literate members of the community. The best theologians are church theologians, those who theologize *from* and *for* the community of faith. They are in one sense the least innovative. In fact, according to some church fathers, innovation is heresy.[3]

But while the leaders help to advance the tradition, it is the community that is the true bearer of the tradition. As a river enlarges

3.   John D. Zizioulas, *Being as Communion* (Crestwood, NY: St Vladimir's Seminary Press, 1993 [1985]), p. 115.

and breaks new grounds as it flows down to the sea yet always remaining one river, so tradition expands and grows as it flows down the stream of time, yet it remains one tradition: it is always identifiable with its source. In the Christian community the source is God himself, who at the Incarnation, 'traditioned' Christ to us. Christ could be said to be the Original Tradition. Christ in turn appointed apostles to carry on what he began. The church subsequently 'canonized' the writings of the apostles, recognizing that they were the first and direct witnesses of the First Tradition, Christ himself. This is what makes the Canon special: it is the embodiment of the First Tradition.

In light of the nature of the Christian tradition we can now understand why Karl Barth is recognized as one of the greatest theologians, if not the greatest theologian, of the twentieth century. His theology is not innovation, but *church* dogmatics, written from the church and for the church, which develops out of the sheer givenness of revelation.[4] Almost a generation after his death, we are seeing something of a revival of his work. His work is original in the sense it helps to expand the Christian tradition, enabling the river to break new ground without causing it to flow into stagnant pools or creating new, independent channels; yet at the same time he makes us feel perfectly at home in the faith of our fathers. He would not be the great theologian that he was if he had simply repeated the past. Barth offers the Pentecostal prophet, pastor and theologian an important object lesson which we will return to at the end.

The Problems of Pentecostal Traditioning

At first glance, one might wonder if Pentecostals have a tradition or need one. Tradition implies *historical* transmission, and the Pentecostal faith has always involved a vertical encounter with Christ through the

4. Right at the very beginning of his *Church Dogmatics* Barth understands theology as the church's talk about God which corresponds to the being of the church. The being of the church is Jesus Christ, the 'heavenly Head' of the church. Theology is not talk about itself, not a reflection on some general religious experience, but about the Christ who indwells the church and gives the church its being. (*Church Dogmatics* I.1 [trans. G.W. Bromiley; Edinburgh: T. and T. Clark, 1975], pp. 4, 100-124). Barth's stress on the givenness of revelation has given rise to Bonhoeffer's charge of 'the positivist doctrine of revelation'. See his *Letters and Papers from Prison* (ed. Eberhard Bethge; trans. Reginald H. Fuler; New York: Macmillan, 1966), p. 168.

Spirit coming from beyond history. Can such an existential, a-historical encounter be adequately transmitted through history? Will not talking about it reduce it to just an object of thought? The problem posed here is similar to that found in mysticism. The mystical experience is by nature ineffable, yet the mystic needs to talk about it; for it is in naming the experience, often using the language of tradition, that one could make any sense of it. 'The mystic must speak the language of the tradition in order to be understood at all.'[5] Similarly, Pentecostals do have a tradition, even if many of them are avowedly opposed to the idea. Whenever a movement seeks to perpetuate itself, it evolves ways of passing on their way of life by means of a system of beliefs and rituals. And Pentecostals are no exception. The issue is not whether they have a tradition, but whether they have been effective in traditioning. Without effective traditioning Pentecostals cannot ensure that what they have experienced will be faithfully handed down to the next generation. If Pentecostals are to maintain their vitality as a movement and hope for their children to catch the same Pentecostal fire, they must think of how best they could pass on their faith more or less in the way that they themselves have experienced it, and yet in a way that takes account of the new context of a new generation of the faithful.

Indications are that Pentecostal traditioning has been strong in some respects and weak in others. The strength of Pentecostal traditioning lies in its powerful narratives. Through their 'testimonies' of God's great work Pentecostals have quite successfully spread their experience to the masses particularly among the poor and unlettered. This 'pedagogy among the oppressed' has the 'potential' of creating large-scale social change.[6] But its weakness lies in its inability to explain itself. Critical self-reflection is essential when a movement matures. Unfortunately, for much of their history Pentecostals have been better at telling their story than explaining it to their children. This is seen in the fact that basic doctrines like baptism in the Spirit have been

5.   Bernard McGinn, *The Foundation of Mysticism: Origin to the Twelfth Century*. I. *The Presence of God: A History of Western Mysticism* (London: SCM Press, 1991), p. 335. Here McGinn is discussing the theory of the scholar of Jewish mysticism, Gershom Scholem. Scholem sees a dialectical relationship between the mystic and the society from which the mystic draws his linguistic resources.

6.   Cheryl Bridges-Johns, *Pentecostal Formation: A Pedagogy among the Oppressed* (Sheffield: Sheffield Academic Press, 1993), pp. 81, 87-91.

formulated in a rather restrictive manner. Peter Hocken has shown that the *experience* of early Pentecostals with regard to this central belief was far richer than the doctrine that was formulated later to explain it. Experientially, Spirit-baptism was a powerful 'revelation' by the Spirit who brings the believer into a new relationship with the triune God.[7] In Hocken's own words, 'There is a kind of Trinitarian procession leading from the Father through the Spirit to the revelation of the Son, who through the Spirit shows us the Father and leads us to him.'[8] Similarly, Macchia in a couple of extensive essays understands Spirit-baptism as a 'theophany' or in-breaking of the eschatological Spirit in extraordinary and new ways.[9] Yet in the Pentecostal doctrinal statements Spirit-baptism was reduced to empowerment for life and service. Recent Pentecostal scholars like Stronstad and Menzies have argued that empowerment for mission was indeed the Lukan understanding of receiving the Spirit,[10] but it could not be said to represent the entire New Testament teaching on the subject. We will take this matter up later.

Another instance of weak traditioning is the discrepancy between the Pentecostal use of the Scripture and their official statement about the nature of Scripture. The official view of Scriptural inerrancy is copied rather uncritically from the fundamentalists, but as Steven Land has observed their practice reveals a much more dynamic view. Their experience of Scripture is that of 'Spirit-Word'—not only the written Word but a Spirit-illuminated, spoken Word.[11] This is much more akin to Barth than to Warfield. Scripture, according to Barth, is not itself revelation, but an authoritative witness to or vehicle of God's revelation. The Word of revelation exists in a dialectical relationship to the words of Scripture.[12] The fact that some later Pentecostals went on

---

7. Hocken, 'Meaning and Purpose', pp. 126-33.

8. Hocken, 'Meaning and Purpose', p. 131.

9. Macchia, 'Sighs Too Deep for Words', pp. 47-73; 'Tongues as a Sign: Towards a Sacramental Understanding of Pentecostal Experience', *Pneuma* 15.1 (Spring 1993), pp. 61-76.

10. Roger Stronstad, *The Charismatic Theology of St Luke* (Peabody, MA: Hendricksen Press, 1984), pp. 63-73; Robert P. Menzies, *Empowered for Witness: The Spirit in Luke–Acts* (Sheffield: Sheffield Academic Press, 1994), esp. pp. 173-201.

11. Land, *Pentecostal Spirituality*, p. 100.

12. For an evangelical understanding of the Barthian view of Scripture, see Donald Bloesch, *A Theology of Word and Spirit* (Downers Grove, IL: InterVarsity

to formulate a doctrine which sharply distinguishes between the *logos*-word and the *rhema*-word shows that, at least, their understanding of Scripture exceeded their wooden inerrancy doctrine, even though their *rhema*-word was to give them no small trouble.[13] Barth's dynamic understanding of revelation would have provided a more adequate conceptual scheme for formulating their own doctrine of Scripture. But how many Pentecostals then as now knew of Barth or appreciated him?

Yet another instance where Pentecostal self-understanding falls short of actual practice is in the area of ecumenism especially in North America. The ecumenical nature of the Pentecostal movement has been well established by Cecil M. Robeck, Jr.[14] Robeck notes that the earliest Pentecostal leaders were 'almost universally' ecumenical in their outlook. But 'our initial vision...slowly began to decay, turning in upon itself, becoming increasingly defensive, pessimistic, compromising, and protectionistic'. Robeck further observes that 'we Pentecostals are ecumenical, we just don't know about it'. Inadequate theology about the nature of Christian unity plus their own cultural baggage led many Pentecostals to be highly selective in their ecumenical endeavours, aligning themselves rather uncritically with the National Association of Evangelicals while—just as uncritically—repudiating relationship with the 'liberal' grouping, the World Council of Churches altogether.[15]

Pentecostals encounter a number of problems in the traditioning process. First, many classical Pentecostals have evolved an anti-tradition rhetoric which consciously pits 'tradition' against the spontaneous and novel work of the Spirit. They have tended to stress their difference with other Christians rather than their similarities, the discontinuities rather than the continuities. For instance, the language of

Press, 1992), pp. 76-81, 184-211. C.S. Lewis's view of Scripture comes amazingly close to Barth's. See Michael J. Christensen, *C.S. Lewis on Scripture* (London: Hodder & Stoughton, 1979).

13. *Rhema*-word comes to be identified with the word of faith of the Positive Confession movement. For a critical evaluation of this movement, see D.R. McConnell, *A Different Gospel: A Historical and Biblical Analysis of the Modern Faith Movement* (Peabody, MA: Hendrickson Press, 1988).

14. Cecil M. Robeck, Jr, 'Name and Glory: The Ecumenical Challenge', in Harold D. Hunter (ed.), *Pastoral Pentecostal-Charismatic Movement* (Cleveland, TN: Society of Pentecostal Studies, 1983); *idem*, 'Taking Stock of Pentecostalism: The Personal Reflections of a Retiring Editor', *Pneuma* 15.1 (Spring 1993), pp. 35-60.

15. Robeck, 'Taking Stock', pp. 39, 44.

'newness' occurs with increasing frequency among Pentecostal-charismatics in recent years. 'God is doing a *new* thing'—that watchword may be their way of legitimating their special identity, but it has also tended to convey an implicit negative message to themselves about the nature of the Christian tradition itself. Yet, Pentecostals are traditional in an unconscious way. That is to say, although they have not reflected deeply on the whys and hows of their faith and experience they have felt the need to perpetuate their experience and defend it against negative evaluations coming mostly from those they are most closely identified with, namely, the evangelicals. Practices are passed on ritually with a minimum of explanation, as reflected in another early watchword: 'Pentecost is not a creed but an experience.' One unfortunate result of this kind of rhetoric is that anything that looks Protestant and charismatic is accepted almost without question. Richard Lovelace has noted the tendency of some Pentecostals to 'seize upon every group which legitimized tongues-speaking as an honorable precursor', thus putting themselves with rather 'strange company' including heretical Spirit-movements like the Cathari, Brethren of the Free Spirit and Ranters.[16] This situation, unfortunately, has not changed since. For example, the way in which many of our Assemblies of God ministers have followed one another to catch the 'Toronto Blessing' is truly astounding. I know of a number of pastors in Singapore who went to Toronto hoping perhaps to get something to kick-start their own church into some kind of revival. The net result of a Toronto pilgrimage is usually two to four weeks of 'holy laughter' and then back to exactly where they had been before they began. There is a real danger for Pentecostals to latch on to a questionable tradition and further dissipate the Pentecostal heritage.

A second problem with Pentecostal traditioning is that it is mostly oral rather than written.[17] There is a certain vitality in oral traditioning. In telling the story, the truth is kept alive. That is the peculiar strength of the practice of giving 'testimonies' in Pentecostal churches. The truth does not exist as 'dead letter' but 'indwells' (to use a term from

16. Richard Lovelace, 'Baptism in the Holy Spirit and the Evangelical Tradition', *Pneuma* 7.2 (Fall 1985), pp. 101-124 (101).

17. Walter Hollenweger lists oral liturgy and narrative tradition as two of the five main characteristics of Pentecostalism. See Jones, Wainwright and Yarnold (eds.), *The Study of Spirituality*, pp. 551-52.

Michael Polanyi)[18] believers in a lively manner. Pentecostalism retains its dynamism precisely because truth is encountered and retold in this simple and direct way. But Pentecostals often fear that when the reality is reflected upon and conceptualized it loses its dynamism. But oral traditioning is no longer effective in a world that has rapidly moved on from an oral-aural culture to a print culture and from print to visual and electronic 'sensoria'.[19] In less than a generation, school children growing up with the electronic calculator have lost the capacity to make simple mental calculations while children growing up memorizing the multiplication table were able to do so as a matter of course. Modern people are so used to instant recall of electronically-stored information that they have lost the capacity for remembrance. They have a short memory—which means that they never learned from the past. They survive on the latest religious fashion which gives them a feeling of newness and hence the delusion that they are making progress.

Thus despite the apprehension about theological reflection, Pentecostals still need to reflect and theologize if they are to ensure that the Pentecostal reality is to be bequeathed to the next generation basically intact. If the first ten years represent the heart of Pentecostalism we need to find out why and how it could be recaptured for subsequent generations. Steven Land's *Pentecostal Spirituality* is a good start in that direction.

The Need for Systematization

But more work needs to be done. For one thing, how do we conceptualize an experience without losing its inner dynamism for the community? The difficulty is that we seem hardly able to think about truth without turning it into an 'object' of our thought and so finding ourselves distanced from it. This is what makes the early Pentecostals fearful of theology and theological seminaries. This point is reflected in the history of theological education in the Assemblies of God, USA. Its

18. For an exposition of Polanyi's concept of indwelling and its importance for interpretation see John C. Puddefoot, 'Indwelling: Formal and Non-Formal Elements in Faith and Life', in Thomas F. Torrance (ed.), *Belief in Science and in Christian Life* (Edinburgh: Hansel Press, 1980), pp. 28-48.

19. For a study of the switch from oral to print culture and its effects see Walter Ong, *The Presence of The Word: Some Prolegoumena for Cultural and Religious History* (New Haven: Yale University Press, 1967).

M.Div. level seminary was for many years called the Assemblies of God Graduate School. Its change of name to 'Theological Seminary' may indicate that the denomination has now come to see theological education as less threatening, if not respectable. But Frank Macchia in a recent essay has noted that at the Assemblies of God Theological Seminary (AGTS) there is still no chair in systematic theology, that no courses in systematic theology are required although there are required courses in biblical theology.[20] One can only conclude that the real importance and function of systematic or dogmatic theology are still not fully appreciated or well understood.

The term systematic theology can be understood in various ways. For much of Christian history theology could not have been other than 'systematic' theology in that it always presupposes the unity of the Scripture and the God of revelation who gives us his Word. At least this was the way theology had been understood right up to the seventeenth century. In the first twelve centuries theology was simply a *habitus* or disposition involving a systematic and prayerful reflection on God from which one obtains 'spiritual knowledge',[21] or as Edward Farley puts it, 'a salvifically oriented knowledge of divine things'.[22] Or, sometimes theology was understood simply as the communication of the direct experience of God. Thus Simeon the New Theologian (949–1022) was so called because he 'communicated a new experience of God'.[23] Even in the mediaeval period when theology was seen more as a science, along with other science like art, law and medicine, it was still very much a unitary discipline—unified around the object of its quest, God. In fact, theology was 'the queen of the sciences' because of the singular importance of its subject matter. Theology was at the top of a unified

20. Frank D. Macchia, 'Pentecostal Theology'. The article is to appear in the revised edition of the *Dictionary of Pentecostal and Charismatic Movements* (Grand Rapids, MI: Zondervan).

21. 'Spiritual knowledge' according to an early Greek father Diadochos of Photiki (400–486), comes from 'the single and simple perceptive faculty...implanted in the soul by the Holy Spirit'. See 'On Spiritual Knowledge and Discrimination: One Hundred Texts', §25 in *The Philokalia*, I (trans. G.E.H. Palmer, Philip Sherrard, Kallistos Ware; London: Faber and Faber, 1979).

22. Edward Farley, *Theologia: The Fragmentation and Unity of Theological Education* (Philadelphia: Fortress Press, 1983), p. 33. The following brief historical excursus is based largely on Farley, pp. 29-48.

23. Ives Congar, *I Believe in the Holy Spirit*, I (3 vols.; trans. David Smith; New York: Seabury Press, 1983), p. 93.

field of knowledge.[24] But nowadays systematic theology is commonly understood to be *one* of the theological disciplines alongside of biblical, pastoral, practical theologies (note the plural), etc. The dispersion of theology into many 'sciences' was, ironically, the result of a view of theology promoted by the Pietists in the late seventeenth century. Pietism's concern for a *practical* theology was understandable in the light of a cut-and-dried Protestant scholasticism prevailing in Europe at that time. But the unintended consequence was the radical reconception of the nature of theology itself. Instead of seeing theology as a unitary science concerning its central 'object' God, the knowledge of whom is an end in itself, the Pietists came to see theology as a deposit of truth which has certain practical applications beyond itself. Farley sums up the situation well:

> It is true that the pietists downplay the doctrinal and polemical aspects of theological study and put more emphasis on Scripture and practical theology. At the same time, they alter the genre of *theologia* from a practical *habitus* or disposition to a content, and once that is done, the problem is immediately created of discerning practical *ends* beyond theology, and the means of obtaining those ends. With this shift, theory-practice in the modern sense is born. For once theology is thought of as itself simply a deposit, a collection of truths, the modern problem of building a bridge from those truth to practical ends is created.[25]

The concern for practical application means that theology is no longer regarded as an end in itself (that is, as 'spiritual knowledge'), but a *study* to inculcate some practical end such as ministerial formation. Once theology is understood in this way, it becomes purely instrumental, a means to serve a higher practical end.[26] This is the way that systematic theology is now generally understood—not a very useful subject in itself unless some practical end could be cited to

---

24. It might be of interest to note here that it is this mediaeval sense of a unified science that the theologian Thomas F. Torrance is seeking to recover using the theories of the 'new physics' developed especially by the scientist-philosopher Michael Polanyi. See, for example, his *Theological Science* (London: Oxford University Press, 1969). Torrance speaks of the knowledge of God as something that arises from reflection on the sheer givenness of God's reality 'bearing upon my experience and thought so powerfully that I cannot but be convinced of His overwhelming reality and rationality' (p. ix). In short, theology grows out of spirituality.

25. Farley, *Theologia*, p. 61 (italics original).

26. Farley, *Theologia*, pp. 59-60.

justify its study. No wonder it is not given very high priority, since it is often seen as a step removed from biblical theology which is thought to be closer to the Bible.

The fact of the matter is that biblical theology is not any more 'biblical' than systematic theology. Historically, it grew out of a period of European history when theology was no longer considered 'the queen of the sciences' but simply another academic discipline. The presuppositions of biblical theology could in fact be naturalistic presuppositions where the issue of 'truth' is bracketed. All the biblical theologian *as* biblical theologian is concerned with is how the different parts of the Bible could be understood in their own historical-cultural settings.

Something more is involved when the church refers to the unity of the Bible at least up to the late seventeenth century. Their belief in the Bible's unity presupposes some kind of divine superintendence of the Bible, so that a truth in one part of Scripture does not exist in isolation but is reflected in the totality of Scripture. This was the rationale for the mediaeval four-fold sense of Scripture. It was the presupposition for carrying on 'spiritual reading' or *lectio divina*. We see this exemplified in *The Way of a Pilgrim*, a story that came out of nineteenth-century Russia about an anonymous pilgrim who discovered the secret of the Jesus Prayer. The entire New Testament, according to the teacher of the pilgrim, is unified around its teaching on prayer.[27]

> Do you see in what marvellous way [prayer] is distributed in all four Evangelists? In St. Matthew we see the introduction to prayer, the form, and the conditions; in St. Mark we find examples; in St. Luke, parables; and in St. John, the mysterious exercise of interior prayer; though either briefly or comprehensively this is presented in all four evangelists. The Acts present the practice and the results of prayer and the Letters and the Revelation the many aspects of the act of prayer.[28]

All this is not to say that we should abandon the historical-critical study of the Bible in order to be spiritual. In so far as the Bible is a historical book, it must be studied in its cultural-historical context. Our God is the God of history. At the same time we must not suppose that the only meaning of Scripture is the one deriving from a literal interpretation of the texts. There is still something to be said for the

27. Anon, *The Way of a Pilgrim and The Pilgrim Continues His Way* (trans. Helen Bacovcin; New York: Image Books, 1978), pp. 131-35.
28. *The Way of a Pilgrim*, p. 134.

mediaeval concept of the *sensus plenum* of Scripture as long as it does not lead to an unrestrained kind of allegorization which ignores the literal sense.[29] Thomas Aquinas, for example, links the fuller, spiritual sense of Scripture to the fact that it is the meaning intended by the author—God. So, while there is a literal-historical sense of Scripture, the things to which the literal words point are themselves pointers to larger, spiritual realities which are intended by God, the author of Scripture. In this way, Thomas grounds the spiritual sense on the literal. Since God is the author of Scripture, the spiritual sense presupposes that the Bible must be understood as a whole and not merely as separate historical texts.[30] What we need is to re-acquire the patristic and mediaeval understanding of theology as a spiritual disposition and a unitary discipline. The very act of reflecting on Scripture which reveals God and who he is leads us to true 'spiritual knowledge'. Such knowledge is an end in itself. The pre-Enlightenment theologians knew of no separation between 'head' knowledge and 'heart' knowledge. There is only one unified knowledge of God, and it gives eternal life (Jn 17.3).

In recent years, this sense of the unity of the Bible is once again finding its place in biblical scholarship through the 'canonical approach' developed by Brevard S. Childs.[31] Like the ancient study of Scripture, canonical hermeneutics seeks to discover the biblical message from the Canon as it stands rather than from the historical construction of the biblical texts—a construction which is often based on very slender historical evidence. What comes through in this approach is that unified patterns of Scripture become important for determining the authoritative biblical message. In other words, what determines a teaching as 'biblical' is not necessarily the result of collating so many proof-texts, but the discovery of the larger pattern of meaning in the whole of Scripture. In the past, this function was fulfilled by traditional dogmatics.

But even systematic theology in the modern sense still retains an

---

29. For a critique of the one-meaning theory of interpretation and a qualified acceptance of typological interpretation see Stephen E. Fowl, *Engaging Scripture: A Model for Theological Interpretation* (Oxford: Basil Blackwell, 1998), pp. 33-40, 56-61.

30. See David C. Steinmetz, 'The Superiority of Pre-Critical Exegesis', in Stephen E. Fowl (ed.), *The Theological Interpretation of Scripture* (Oxford: Basil Blackwell, 1997), pp. 26-38.

31. See his *Biblical Theology of the Old and New Testaments* (Minneapolis, MN: Fortress Press, 1993).

important feature which might well serve as the starting point for a return to an earlier understanding of theology as 'spiritual knowledge'. Systematic theology is by nature an integrative theological science. Its basic presupposition is the unity of the Bible. The tendency to systematize was not due to the natural human penchant for neatness; it grew out of a deeply spiritual impulse regarding the nature of the Bible. The construals of systematic theology are the result of integrating the various strands of historical revelation on a common theme. The Trinity is an example of a systematic construal. There are no proof-texts for the Trinity,[32] and attempts to use them may not get us any nearer to the biblical teaching about the nature of God, as the ancient trinitarian controversy between Athanasius and Arius showed. Arius had plenty of proof-texts while Athanasius had few. What made the Athanasian trinitarian doctrine biblical (i.e. authoritative) is the discovery of the larger pattern of meaning of Scripture viewed as a unity concerning the self-revelation of God. It was faithfulness to the whole structure of God's self-revelation that clinched the argument for Athanasius.[33] The Trinity is not an attempt at explaining the inner nature of God in terms of some divine mathematics that transcends ordinary logic. Rather, the carefully contrived terms—one being (*ousia*) and three persons (*hypostases*)—are the way the church attempts to state faithfully in the light of that revelation the parameters for correct belief about God (orthodoxy). Within these basic terms of reference, one could then go on to discuss the nature of the relationship between the Persons: the *perichoresis*. Here, differences in emphasis between the Eastern and Western church appear, but these differences are set within the bounds of a common orthodoxy. The Trinity, then, could be said to establish the canonical meaning of Scripture concerning God.

What we see in the doctrine of the Trinity extends to the rest of the basic beliefs of the church as embodied, for example, in the ecumenical creeds. In other words, it is through systematic reflection on Scripture that the church understands its own relationship with God and the true nature of its existence. The creeds ensure that the church's basic

32. No less a theologian than Karl Barth, who more than any other had helped modern Christians to return to the doctrine of the Trinity, concedes as much. See *Church Dogmatics* I.1, p. 375.

33. By contrast, Arianism represented the imposition of human reason on divine revelation. See Charles J. Scalise, *From Scripture to Theology: A Canonical Journey into Hermeneutics* (Downers Grove, IL: InterVarsity Press, 1996), p. 86.

identity is faithfully transmitted through history. The traditioning of the faith is by a process of systematic reflection on the Bible understood not so much as a collection of texts but as canonical Scripture. We shall see in Chapter 2 how this is applied to the traditioning of the central beliefs of Pentecostalism.

The systematic reflection on Scripture is not 'academic' but prayerful. At least this was the way all systematic theology had been undertaken by the church up to the late seventeenth century when the Cartesian methodology began to supplant the holistic way of understanding truth. Up to that time, the truth about God was, as we have already noted, simply 'spiritual knowledge', that is, knowledge which 'unites man to God through experience'.[34] No matter how abstruse the discussion about God may be, the end is always relationship with God. The idea that truth could be 'merely intellectual' never crossed the minds of these theologians, even though by today's reckoning their discussion would be considered highly speculative. In fact, for them, to 'speculate' means to behold the truth as in a mirror (*speculum*). The picture is derived from 2 Cor. 3.18 which reads in the Vulgate: '*Nos vero omnes, revelata facie gloriam Domini speculantes…*'[35] Similarly, 'intellect' had a meaning quite different from what it has today. For the early Greek bishop Diadochos of Photiki, the intellect is the 'perceptive faculty' of the soul which is indwelled by the Holy Spirit at baptism. Diadochos repeatedly stresses the function of the intellect as the means to gain spiritual knowledge through the 'remembrance of God'.[36] Truth is never divorced from life or confined to one aspect of the mind, the rational faculty. St Anselm's *Proslogion* is another classic example of this holistic way of thinking about truth. We are all familiar with his 'ontological argument' for the existence of God. Perhaps what most of us do not know is that for Anselm it was not just an abstruse piece of logic which Kant finally managed to dislodge. It was for Anselm a deeply felt truth which he presented in the form of a prayer.

> Something than which nothing greater can be thought so truly exists that it is not possible to think of it as not existing.

---

34. Diadochos, 'On Spiritual Knowledge', §9 in *The Philokalia*, I.

35. Cf. the way Diadochos understands the work of the 'theologian' as that involving the 'contemplative faculty' or 'divine speculation' to arrive at a state of 'dispassion' (§77).

36. Diadochos, 'On Spiritual Knowledge', §32, 36, 58, 59, 79, 81.

This being is yourself, our Lord and God. Lord my God, you so truly are, that it is not possible to think of you as not existing. And rightly so. For if someone's mind could think of something better than you, the creature would rise higher than its creator and would judge its creator; which is clearly absurd. For whatever exists except you alone can be thought of as not existing. Therefore you alone of all most truly are, and you exist most fully of all things.[37]

For Anselm, knowing about God and knowing God are one and the same thing. He knows nothing about any 'abstract' thought about God based on pure reasoning. Understanding God is always in the context of a believing heart: *Credo ut intelligam* ('I believe in order that I may understand').

The point I am making here about pre-Enlightenment theology goes back to a problem posed earlier: How do we reflect on the truth without losing its total reality? We can see that the danger of turning truth into merely an object of thought is itself a modern problem. The modern mind is still very much possessed by the Cartesian ghost which instinctively tells it that thinking about something or someone must involve a subject 'I' acting on an object 'it'. The moment we 'objectivize' something we see it less than whole. So when modern Christians speak piously of cultivating 'heart' knowledge and derogatorily of 'head' knowledge, little do they realize that their understanding of theology already presupposes the Cartesian epistemology rather than the holistic faith of the church.

The Place for Spiritual Theology

But there is a way to think about truth without reducing its vitality. It is by a method which the larger Christian tradition calls spiritual theology. Spiritual theology is a way of training our minds to refocus on the truth so that the truth comes alive. It seeks a return to holistic thinking.[38] Thinking about God and praying to God are not two discrete acts which

---

37. Anselm, *Prayers and Meditations of St Anselm with the Proslogion* (trans. Benedicta Ward; London: Penguin Books, 1973), p. 245.

38. It is noteworthy that spiritual theology as a distinctive sub-discipline of theology developed about the same time when theology was fragmented into different branches. In a sense, spiritual theology as a discipline concedes to this de facto fragmentation, but takes as its special task to reintegrate the theological disciplines.

we must somehow try to bring together by some mechanical bridge called 'spiritual application'; rather, they are ultimately a single act of relating to God. If Pentecostals in the early twenty-first century are to recover the heart of the movement in the first ten years, they need to develop a Pentecostal spiritual theology.

A Pentecostal spiritual theology must satisfy three conditions. First, it must not shrink from thinking through the Pentecostal's basic belief and experience with exactitude and thoroughness. The way back to holistic thinking must begin at least with a theological method that is systematic and integrative. This integrative approach requires Pentecostals to relate the distinctively Pentecostal experience to the larger Christian spiritual tradition. Pentecostals are often fearful that their own distinctiveness would be lost if it is interpreted within the larger tradition. But it is more likely to be lost among the enthusiastic fringe cults if it does not negotiate within the mainstream of Christian tradition. The reason for this is quite obvious. Whether we are Pentecostal, Protestant, Catholic or Orthodox we are all trinitarians (at least most of us are, with the exception of the oneness Pentecostals). And this means that our understanding of the work of the Spirit, no matter how different it may be from our non-Pentecostal brethren, cannot be too far divorced from the Spirit's relationship to the Father and the Son. Pentecostals can contribute to a richer understanding of and experience with the triune God by focusing on the distinctive role of the Spirit. We think best as Pentecostals if we think in the context of the trinitarian faith rather than apart from it.

To reflect upon the nature of the Spirit's work in the Trinity is to discover the point of integration between belief and practice in the affection. This point has been well brought out by Steven Land.[39] The Spirit, following Augustine's understanding of the Trinity, is the bond of love between the Father and the Son and between Christ and the church. Pentecostal spirituality which looks at the Trinity from the perspective of the Spirit, could then be characterized by a special configuration of religious affections (orthopathy) which enlivens right belief (orthodoxy) and issues in right practice (orthopraxy). Orthopathy is the 'personal integrating center of orthodoxy and orthopraxy'.[40]

---

39. Land, *Pentecostal Spirituality*, pp. 41-47, 122-81, ch. 3.
40. Land, *Pentecostal Spirituality*, p. 44.

Affections, according to Jonathan Edwards,[41] are what true religion in great part consists of. True religious affections are not any kind of emotions, not even a profusion of intense emotions, but have to be 'gracious' or 'saving' affections. They have to be shaped by the gospel and grow out of the gospel story. This is particularly important from the standpoint of spiritual discernment. The truth or falsity of a religious faith is to be tested not so much by right belief or right practice alone, but essentially by how the beliefs and practices are integrated and manifested through gracious affections. The Pharisees held orthodox beliefs and observed correct practices by keeping meticulously close to the demands of the law. But they lacked true affections. Jesus, who discerned what was in the human heart (Jn 2.24), saw their hypocrisy and lack of love (Lk. 11.39, 42). Pentecostal spirituality is essentially affective trinitarianism.

The Pentecostal religious affections can only be rightly exercised within a trinitarian context. Conversely, some of the problems and excesses among Pentecostal-charismatics in recent years can be attributed to a lack of proper grounding in the Trinity. A case in point can be seen in the fixation on power, signs and wonders and the demonic among influential leaders of the 'Third Wave' such as Peter Wagner and Charles Kraft. This problem can be traced to the failure to understand the hiddenness of the Spirit as the basic structure of the trinitarian relationship. Tom Smail calls the Spirit 'the person without a face'.[42] Smail is right when he says, 'A spirit who offers us experience of himself and his gifts as the central focus of our Christian life is not the Holy Spirit of the New Testament.'[43] Spiritual gifts are not about the Spirit, but about God who reveals himself in the gifts. Even when Paul discusses the charisms in 1 Cor. 12, where we would expect a stronger focus on the Spirit's activity, we see, rather, the gifts interpreted within a trinitarian context. Paul indeed calls the gifts 'the manifestation of the Spirit' (v. 7), that is, 'a disclosure of the Spirit's activity',[44] yet such a manifestation is clearly subsumed under the unity of God (vv. 4-6). As Fee points out, the activity of the Spirit is

41. *The Religious Affections* (Edinburgh: Banner of Truth, 1986 [1796]), p. 23.

42. Tom Smail, *The Giving Gift: The Holy Spirit in Person* (London: Hodder & Stoughton, 1988), pp. 30-55.

43. Smail, *The Giving Gift*, p. 64.

44. Gordon Fee, *God's Empowering Presence: The Holy Spirit in the Letters of Paul* (Peabody, MA: Hendricksen Press, 1994), p. 164.

'functionally subordinated' to the Father. Ultimately, it is God who gives the gifts through the Spirit.[45]

The Spirit who is the bond of the love in the intra-trinitarian life could also be described as its invisible glue.[46] The Christian tradition is quite consistent in affirming the Spirit's hiddenness. The Spirit is not the *direct* focus of our worship. The Nicene Creed identifies the Spirit as one 'who together with the Father and the Son is worshipped and glorified'. The church has kept to the spirit of Creed by composing few songs in direct praise of or petition to the Spirit.[47] Mostly, the glorification of the Spirit is set within a strictly trinitarian formula such as the Doxology. Many modern theologians, Pentecostal and non-Pentecostal, have decried the lack of attention given to the Spirit. If there had been a lack, it was not always from sheer negligence but partly for a sound theological reason: it seeks at least to be faithful to a trinitarian understanding of the Spirit. Many Pentecostals fear that putting the Holy Spirit in the background might lead to his ministry being neglected and consequently to an arid Christianity. But recognizing the Spirit's hiddenness is not the same as neglecting the work of the Spirit; rather, it means paying attention to the fact of his hiddenness. Giving due recognition to this truth, far from watering down the Pentecostal message, it actually preserves it from abuse by extremists at both ends: those who are obsessed with supernatural gifts and those who are obsessed with denying them. If the doctrine of the hiddenness of the Spirit is taken seriously it will actually produce a balanced Pentecostal. A balanced Pentecostal is one who speaks in tongues, prays for the sick, casts out demons without paying much attention to any of these things in and of themselves. He or she is intensely concerned with what the Spirit himself is intensely concerned with, namely, the glorification of Christ. The Spirit is truly glorified precisely when the Father and Son are glorified. *That* understanding must become a basic part of Pentecostal spirituality.

The second condition that a Pentecostal spiritual theology must meet is that the life in the Spirit cannot be divorced from the church, the Body of Christ. The Spirit as the agent of integration between belief and practice also integrates believers in the Body of Christ. I will take

45. Fee, *God's Empowering Presence*, p. 163.
46. Augustine, *De Trinitate* 15.27.
47. The ancient hymn, *Veni, Sancte Spiritus* (Come, Holy Spirit) is one such rare exception.

up this theme later. What I would like to do here is to consider the work of the Spirit in the traditioning process. The popular notion that the Spirit is opposed to tradition could not have been further from the truth. One can understand how such a notion would arise. The Spirit spells freedom and spontaneity, and nothing could be more contrary to the Spirit than a rigid and dead traditionalism.

But tradition understood as the on-going work of the Spirit in the church is far from dead. It is an active process of handing down the church's common life, belief and practices. More precisely, it is by the Spirit given by Christ to the church and indwelling the church that the church becomes a traditioning body. The Spirit's uniting the church to Christ who is the Truth becomes the basis for affirming the continuity of Christ, Scripture and Tradition. The living tradition of the church is an extension of the primary Tradition of the Father's gift of Son and his Holy Spirit.[48] The Son who sends the Spirit to indwell the church is himself the subject of the Spirit's illumination in the church. The Spirit's work in the church, therefore, is not restricted to authenticating the Scripture (which is what is normally understood in evangelical circles). The Spirit continues his work as the Spirit of revelation to enable the church to know Christ better (Eph. 1.17), but always in keeping with what has already gone before: the primary revelation of Christ embodied in sacred Scriptures. Through the Spirit there is an expanding understanding of Christ and the Scripture, but always within the church.

The church, therefore, is the locus of the Spirit's on-going work which could be called the living tradition.[49] Pentecostals who understand the role of the Spirit in the development of the living tradition in the church will be able to avoid the Scylla of a wooden biblicism found among the fundamentalists and the Charybdis of extra-biblical and private revelations of self-styled prophets. Some of the early Pentecostals understood this when, on the one hand, they refused to put the creeds above the 'Spirit-Word of Scripture', and on the other, were concerned about the need to define sound doctrine clearly. Frank Bartleman exemplified the first concern, while William Seymour the latter.[50]

48. Father Andrew (Isaac Melton), 'A Response to Harold O.J. Brown', in James S. Cutsinger (ed.), *Reclaiming the Great Tradition* (Downers Grove, IL: InterVarsity Press, 1997), p. 91.

49. Smail, *The Giving Gift*, pp. 74-75.

50. Land, *Pentecostal Spirituality*, pp. 105-108.

Thirdly, if the Pentecostal movement hopes for a vibrant spiritual theology to emerge, it must reconsider its current practice of worship. Worship is probably the most crucial aspect of the church's spiritual life. In worship the church is engaged in a form of communal practice. It is not the only form but probably its most primary form. In worship the church regularly re-enacts its beliefs, that is to say, it practices its beliefs regarding who God is. Worship is essentially practising theology in the proper sense of the word. I am using practice in the way that Alasdair MacIntyre uses the term. MacIntyre defines practice as

> any coherent and complex form of socially established cooperative human activity through which goods internal to that form of activity are realised in the course of trying to achieve those standards of excellence which are appropriate to, and partially definitive of, that form of activity, with the result that human powers to achieve excellence, and human conceptions of the ends and goods involved, are systematically extended.[51]

Worship is that coherent and cooperative, and hence, communal practice involving reenacting certain truths concerning who God is, as a result of which certain virtues are formed. MacIntyre's definition also states that the practice aims at realizing certain 'goods internal to that form of activity'. In worship, the internal good is the strengthening of the relationship between the community with the God it worships. The practice of submitting to God in recognition of his sovereignty and holiness leads to the formation of humility. The practice of thanksgiving in recognition of God's benevolence forms gratitude, etc.[52] There are, of course, other practices of the Christian community, but worship is the primary act as it has to do with the virtues linking the community to God. It is therefore the primary traditioning act, which ensures that the church's primary relational virtues (the Godward theological virtues of faith, hope and charity) are 'systematically extended'.

The critical issue for the Pentecostals is, what are they practising in

---

51. Alisdair MacIntyre, *After Virtue: A Study in Moral Theory* (Notre Dame, IN: University of Notre Dame Press, 1981), p. 175.

52. For a study of the ramifications of MacIntyre's virtue ethics in Christianity, see Nancey Murphy, Brad J. Kallenberg and Mark Thiessen Nation (eds.), *Virtues and Practices in the Christian Tradition* (Harrisburg, PA: Trinity Press International, 1997).

Pentecostal worship? Current models of worship in charismatic and evangelical circles reveal their respective inadequacies. The charismatic model is usually organized around the singing of praises, as seen in the way the contemporary worship service is called: 'prayer and praise' or 'praise and worship'. When worship is largely reduced to a string of praise ditties the aim of worship subtly shifts from encountering God (the 'internal goods') to mood creation and possibly psychological manipulation (the 'external goods').[53] The theological virtues of faith, hope and charity are no longer clearly seen as qualities based on the truth of who God is, but are reduced to psychological states. Worshippers are worked up or are told to work themselves up to have faith for one thing or another, especially healing. They are told that if only they *really* believe, the Lord will answer their prayer, that if they are not healed, it is a sign that they lack faith.

The evangelical model, on the other hand, sometimes suffers from a different kind of reductionism. Here, worship is reduced to preaching. Singing is only a preparation to hear the sermon. The soul-stirring sermon takes the place of the soul-stirring choruses. Reductionistic worship simply practises a reductionistic theology even when the church's theology may be theoretically sound. What, then, makes for a sound, holistic worship which enlivens a sound, holistic theology? I would like to suggest that it is a worship where the eucharist is the organizing centre. I will say more about the nature of the eucharistic community in the last chapter. Here I will only mention the main features of eucharistic worship to show why it should provide the framework for worship.

Evelyn Underhill in her classic text on worship describes the eucharist as 'the greatest of all Christian acts of worship'. It is an act in which 'both natural and supernatural, visible and invisible: the unchanging realities of adoration, oblation, sacrifice, supplication, and communion [are] made more actual and penetrating, not less, by their

---

53. MacIntyre, *After Virtue*, pp. 175-78. In the context of worship, encountering God is an internal good because it is intrinsic to the practice of Christian worship. It is the thing aimed at which extends Christian virtues in worship. Whereas the external good is a 'good' that does not serve the intrinsic aim of worship. It is called an external good only because the person or persons who advance it regard it as a good. They are, according to MacIntyre, 'characteristically objects of competition' (p. 178).

humble outward expression in terms of our temporal experience'.[54] In the eucharist all the basic elements and dimensions of worship find their proper place.[55] It unites both the charismatic and evangelical dimensions of worship into a coherent whole. It is the occasion in which ordinary things (bread and wine) and ordinary historical experience (eating and drinking) are 'transfigured' through the action of the Spirit who is regularly invoked in the eucharistic celebration. The church becomes the charismatic body of Christ through the coming of the Spirit at the Pentecost event and is renewed as a charismatic body as the Spirit is called upon in the epiclesis. This is how the charismatic dimension is maintained. The evangelical dimension, too, is preserved in the celebration of the mystery of the faith: Christ has died, Christ is risen, Christ will come again. Throughout the eucharist, this mystery is celebrated, remembered, re-enacted, reappropriated and applied, besides being proclaimed. Evangelicals, however, have tended to reduce worship to proclamation. The net result is a rather impoverished form of worship involving only the rational dimension of life. If Pentecostals would learn to appropriate the 'practice' of eucharistic worship they will be better equipped to preserve both Spirit and word, praise and proclamation in their distinctively Pentecostal way of life.

Conclusion

What is the future of Pentecostal traditioning? I do not claim any special prophetic insight, but based on the way things are evolving, there is cause for both hope and concern. Hope, in that there is an increasing number of Pentecostal theologians who are doing serious theological reflection on the Pentecostal reality. This has led Hollenweger to comment that Pentecostalism has come of age.[56] But there is also cause for concern because many of these theologians are often shunned and marginalized by their own denominational leadership. Even though the Pentecostal theological fraternity is getting stronger, as long as the role of the theologian is not recognized by his or

54. Evelyn Underhill, *Worship* (Guildford, Surrey: Eagle, 1991 [1936]), pp. 106, 108.

55. Underhill discusses six elements: thanksgiving, memorial, sacrifice, supplication, the mystery of the presence, and the heavenly food (*Worship*, pp. 108-112).

56. Hollenweger, 'The Critical Tradition', p. 17.

her own church, the theologian will not be able to help the church in its traditioning. He or she will remain a voice crying in the wilderness, ignored by the establishment and occasionally silenced. As I have said at the beginning, the real work of traditioning can only be done by *church* theologians doing *church* dogmatics à la Barth. Even though this is difficult for many Pentecostal theologians, they must try, like Barth, to theologize in, from and for the church. The church is that river, the bearer of the tradition. They must help to unclog the river and let it flow freely. They must recognize that their future is with the church: *nulla salus extra ecclesiam* ('no salvation outside the church')! The fault, however, does not always lie with the establishment. The theologian must bear part of the blame. Sometimes theologians are guilty of acting out of a sense of superior knowledge. This will only confirm in the ordinary church members and an insecure denominational leadership that theologians are puffed up. We often hear complaints like 'If that's what theological education does to one, then all the more reason why we should have nothing to do with it!' The emerging Pentecostal community of scholars must find ways to relate meaningfully with their respective ecclesiastical bodies. There is a need to develop trust. For this both theologians and church leaders must return to Paul's teaching in Romans 14 and 15 on the need for mutual respect between the strong and the weak: 'We who are strong [in theological knowledge?] ought to put up with the failings of the weak and not to please ourselves' (Rom. 15.1). Perhaps theologians must first learn to behave properly in deference to the conscience of the weak. Then there is hope for the future.

Chapter 2

GLOSSOLALIA AS 'INITIAL EVIDENCE'

If there is one teaching that appears to have the least support in the larger spiritual tradition it would be glossolalia as the initial evidence of Spirit-baptism. Although more recent studies like McDonnell and Montague's have given the Pentecostal-charismatic experience a wider historical grounding, glossolalia particularly in the way that Pentecostals have understood it, remains highly problematic. It is one thing to show that there was some historical evidence of occurrences of prophetic gifts including tongues,[1] but quite another to show from history that it had the same significance that modern Pentecostals have given to it. No wonder theologically it is becoming something of an embarrassment, even while classical Pentecostals continue to maintain its special place of importance. Increasingly, even ordinary lay people are questioning if it is really that important. When there is no strong theological underpinning for a practice it will eventually fall into disuse. As we have already noted, signs of its practical abandonment are already apparent in Pentecostal churches.

But the case for the Pentecostal doctrine of initial evidence may not be as lost as it appears. Henry Lederle who himself rejected the doctrine, has noted that among most charismatics glossolalia continues to be exercised regularly and even occupies 'a prominent position' in their experience.[2] One must ask the charismatic why practically it is so important when theologically it is relegated to a position of relative insignificance. Does a teaching that regards it as merely one of the signs

---

1. Kilian McDonnell and George T. Montague, *Christian Initiation and Baptism in the Holy Spirit: Evidence from the First Eight Centuries* (Collegeville, MN: Liturgical Press, 1991), p. 323.

2. Lederle, Henry, 'Initial Evidence and the Charismatic Movement: An Ecumenical Appraisal', in Gary G. McGee (ed.), *Initial Evidence: Historical and Biblical Perspectives on the Pentecostal Doctrine of Spirit Baptism* (Peabody, MA: Hendricksen Press, 1991), pp. 131-41 (132).

of Spirit-baptism adequately explain its prominence in charismatic experience? In other words, the way that glossolalia is actually experienced seems to cry out for a better explanation than the one commonly advanced by evangelical charismatics.

The doctrine of 'initial evidence' as it stands is difficult to defend either on the basis of historical evidence or biblical precedents. But I would like to argue that it can be coherently defended if we could establish the logical relationship between glossolalia and Spirit-baptism. Their theological coherence can be established if the doctrine of Spirit-baptism is broadened to incorporate both charismatic and soteriological dimensions. Such an integrated pneumatology shows that Spirit-baptism is better understood primarily in terms of revelation and personal intimacy and only derivatively, as empowerment for mission. Pentecostals seek to capture a unique reality with a unique sign: they see glossolalia as an appropriate symbol of this spiritual reality. Thus, within the Pentecostal community at least, glossolalia as initial evidence makes good sense. It makes even better sense when evidential tongues are interpreted within the broader context of the Christian mystical tradition where silence signals a certain level of intimacy with God. Silence and tongues have the same logical function within the respective communities. At this level it becomes apparent that glossolalia, like silence, bears a much stronger relationship to Spirit-baptism than just being an appropriate symbol. The relationship is of such a kind that one is quite justified to call it 'the initial evidence'. But ultimately, glossolalia makes the best sense when it is understood as signifying a reality which configures gracious and powerful affections in a distinctively Pentecostal way. Its truth must finally be seen in terms of transformed persons and communities.

The problem of evidential tongues has to do with the question of how the relationship between tongues and Spirit-baptism could be meaningfully understood. It is, first, a problem of hermeneutics. It will not do to make a case for it because 'it is there in the Bible'. The early Pentecostal argument for glossolalia as initial evidence is weak because it was based strictly on a straight-forward reading of Acts where in a few instances glossolalia accompanied the phenomenon of being filled with the Spirit. But as Fee has pointed out, establishing a biblical doctrine is not a simple case of following a biblical precedent.[3] But it is not even a

---

3. Gordon Fee, 'Baptism in the Holy Spirit: The Issue of Separability and Subsequence', *Pneuma* 7.2 (Fall 1985), pp. 87-100.

matter of establishing the original intention of the author as Fee himself believes. At this level of understanding, the fact that Luke associates tongues with Spirit-baptism could at most be seen as something 'normal' but not the 'norm', or as one of the signs but not *the* sign of Spirit-baptism.[4] Whether glossolalia can be regarded as normative will always remain an open question.

But Pentecostal scholarship in recent years has moved the debate far beyond the level of naïve biblicism of the early Pentecostals and the authorial intention of evangelical hermeneutics.[5] Robert Menzies, employing Dunn's redactional hermeneutics has argued strongly for a distinctive Lukan pneumatology, focusing on the charismatic gifts, the consistent association of the coming of the Spirit with some kind of inspired speech such as prophecy and tongues, all of which reveal Luke's missiological perspective.[6] Menzies's understanding has no doubt helped to place the relationship of glossolalia and Spirit-filling on a firmer footing. His conclusion turns out to be not very different from that of the Pentecostal pioneers, who had a true instinctual grasp of their experience, even though their explanations were often inadequate. Within early Pentecostalism, there was a view (also found in the Holiness movement) that the filling of the Spirit was for the purpose of preaching the gospel, and tongues were actual foreign languages given for that purpose.[7] Glossolalia was more than a sign; it was the means to

4.   Larry W. Hurtado, 'Normal, but not a Norm: "Initial Evidence" and the New Testament', in McGee (ed.), *Initial Evidence*, pp. 189-201.

5.   E.g. Stronstad, *Charismatic Theology*; Robert Menzies, *The Development of Early Christian Pneumatology with Special Reference to Luke–Acts* (Sheffield: JSOT Press, 1991) and *idem, Empowered for Witness*; James B. Shelton, *Mighty in Word and Deed: The Role of the Holy Spirit in Luke–Acts* (Peabody, MA: Hendrickson, 1991); John Penny, *The Missionary Emphasis of Lukan Pneumatology* (Sheffield: Sheffield Academic Press, 1997).

6.   Menzies, however, has faulted Dunn for not using his method consistently ('Evidential Tongues: An Essay on Theological Method', *Asian Journal of Pentecostal Studies* 1.2 (July 1998), pp. 111-23 (114).

7.   D. William Faupel, 'Glossolalia as Foreign Language: An Investigation of the Early Twentieth-Century Pentecostal Claim', *Wesleyan Theological Journal* 31.1 (Spring 1996), pp. 95-109, see esp. 95-99. Faupel also notes that the Holiness movement later repudiated the Pentecostal claim when it became apparent that the tongues spoken were not foreign languages at all. When evidence against the presence of xenolalia became overwhelming, the Pentecostals too revised their views about the nature of tongues.

fulfilling the great commission. This belief, however, did not survive very long when it became painfully clear to some early Pentecostal missionaries that glossolalia had no resemblance to any kind of foreign language at all. But even if tongues are not foreign languages, they are still an appropriate *symbol* of a spiritual reality whose primary aim (as far as Luke is concerned) is to empower believers to *preach* the gospel across ethnic and linguistic boundaries. Menzies's studies, however, still fall short of showing conclusively that glossolalia is the initial evidence. As I have pointed out elsewhere, at most it shows that some kind of inspired speech, including tongues, is quite central to Luke's pneumatology. But in Luke prophetic speech rather than glossolalia seems to be more prominent. Might not prophecy serve better as evidence than glossolalia?[8]

This criticism, far from invalidating what Menzies has done, only reveals the limits of a strictly biblical theology approach to establishing doctrine. The Pentecostal doctrine can be vindicated if we can establish it within the larger pattern of meaning derived from the whole canon of Scripture, as noted in Chapter 1. But when we speak of a canonical meaning we need to introduce another factor into the interpretive process, namely, the church as the interpretive community. The canon is more than just a motley collection of 66 books. To recognize these books as constituting the canon implies an interpretive process involving the dynamic relationship between the texts and the interpretive community which shapes and is shaped by that body of texts. It is within this interactive process that we can speak of a canonical, authoritative and 'biblical' meaning.[9] Conservative Christians have tended to understand interpretation as involving a one-way process centring on the text, as if there is a single, independent meaning in there waiting to be discovered, which once discovered, will decisively settle the issue. What the canonical approach has helped us to see is that meaning arises from the interaction of Scripture and the interpretive community.[10] This does not mean that the church (here we are thinking of the church in its

---

8. Simon Chan, 'The Language Game of Glossolalia, or Making Sense of the Initial Evidence', in Menzies and Ma (eds.), *Pentecostalism in Context*, pp. 82-83n. See also Max Turner's assessment in 'Tongues: An Experience for All in the Pauline Churches?' *Asian Journal of Pentecostal Studies* 1.2 (July 1998), pp. 231-53.

9. See Scalise, *From Scripture to Theology*, pp. 84-88; Fowl, *Engaging Scripture*, p. 60.

10. Fowl, *Engaging Scripture*, pp. 56-60.

synchronic and diachronic sense) authoritatively determines the true meaning of Scripture, as if meaning has now shifted from the text to the community, as some postmodern interpreters would like us to believe. Rather, we are saying that the church as the canonically shaped community *recognizes* the truth as it embodies or 'indwells' the Scripture, such that the community (the Body of Christ) could be said to be an extension of Scripture. This is a more faithful account of the way Christian doctrine developed than the view that sees truth as residing solely in the texts. The failure to recognize the critical role of the community in the interpretive process is one main reason why biblical scholars on both sides of the debate over tongues and the doctrine of subsequence are not anywhere nearer to resolving the issues.[11]

Just as it is possible to speak of a canonical meaning or meanings of Scripture which is more than the sum total of the meanings of individual texts, as can be seen in the way the classical doctrine of the Trinity was established as a biblical doctrine, the same dynamic is at work when we seek to formulate a doctrine of initial evidence.[12] If Spirit-baptism refers to the coming of the Spirit upon the church to establish a special relationship with the Trinity, and glossolalia is a particular kind of prayer which makes the best sense in the light of that reality, then the biblical explanation of glossolalia will have to take into account a number of teachings, including the nature of revelation (especially theophany), prayer, personal relationship, divine action, etc., and not just the texts where glossolalia and Spirit-baptism are explicitly referred to.[13] There is no reason not to regard such an integrated approach as

11. This is especially true of Pentecostals and Evangelicals. See n. 13 below.

12. This is how Simon Tugwell has sought to understand the Pentecostal experience of glossolalia. According to Tugwell, glossolalia has to be seen in relation to the 'structural whole' of the Pentecostal religion (Simon Tugwell, 'The Speech-Giving Spirit: A Dialogue with Tongues', in *New Heavens? New Earth?* [Springfield, IL: Templegate Publishers, 1976], pp. 119-59 [150]). This approach may explain why Catholic charismatics are generally more sympathetic to the doctrine of initial evidence than evangelicals. They recognize the necessity of seeing the doctrine in relation to the total Pentecostal way of life.

13. The difficulty of establishing doctrines based on interpretation of individual texts is illustrated in the recent exchanges between Max Turner and Robert Menzies on the universality of tongues. See their respective articles in *Asian Journal of Pentecostal Studies* 1.2 (July 1998) and 2.2 (July 1999). In the end the success at establishing the authoritative meaning of the relevant texts in 1 Cor. 14 through historical reconstructions and such like is limited. This is not to minimize the value

biblical. If we adopt this canonical approach, we would then come to see the individual texts in a different way. The texts themselves may not prove conclusively that glossolalia is the initial evidence, but they do serve as pointers to a broader pattern of meaning in Scripture in which the initial evidence doctrine actually makes compelling sense, especially within the Pentecostal community that shapes and is shaped by that pattern of meaning. And so, going back to Menzies's understanding of Lukan pneumatology, textually, prophetic utterances are not the same as glossolalia, but the former are part of a pattern of ecstatic speech that seems to be connected closely with a certain kind of divine manifestation in the Scripture. We must then ask, why is the manifestation of the Spirit particularly associated with speech rather than some other phenomena, like visions and dreams? To answer this question would require an understanding of the canonical meaning of speech and personhood and their relationship, and not just about the *textual* distinction between tongues, prophecy and other forms of ecstatic speech.

The works of Pentecostal scholars like Menzies and others are a good start. They have shown, using the newer sophisticated tools of redactional-critical hermeneutics, that there is more to glossolalia in relation to Spirit-filling in Luke than its just being one of the signs alongside of many others. There is even an inner coherence between ecstatic speech and Spirit-baptism once we accept the missiological emphasis of Luke. But we need to press the issue further and ask whether this Lukan theology which signifies Spirit-baptism with ecstatic speech can be further developed into a doctrine where glossolalia in particular bears a unique relationship to Spirit-baptism. I believe that this can be done if we can show that glossolalia bears a *necessary* relation to Spirit-baptism within the larger pattern of canonical meaning and that Spirit-baptism is an experience involving a special kind of relationship with God.

Relationship is a more basic category for understanding the nature of

of such dialogues but to point out that in the final analysis doctrines are derived from looking at the whole structure of Scripture which shapes and is shaped by the interpretive community. No matter how finely biblical scholars weave their exegetical nets they will not be able to catch the 'truth' as long as there is failure to recognize that what passes as objective or scientific interpretation is actually a pattern of viewing the texts from the perspective of a particular interpretive community. Perhaps it is time for both Pentecostals and Evangelicals to acknowledge freely that in point of fact they inhabit different interpretive communities which account for their different shades of meaning given to the classic 'Pentecostal' texts.

the work of the Spirit than mission. We can understand mission in terms of relationship but not vice versa. Ultimately, mission has to be seen in terms of reconciliation or restoration of the relationship between God and the world and the creation of a new community in Christ. That is to say, if glossolalia is related to mission in any way, it is related to it in the sense that the speaking in other tongues (as happened on the day of Pentecost) *symbolically* brings people of every nation, tribe and tongue together to form the new people of God and reverses the confusion of tongues that occurred at the Tower of Babel.[14] Evidential tongues will have to be established on a broader understanding of tongues and Spirit-baptism which comes from integrating the various strands of New Tetstament pneumatology into the pattern of canonical meaning.[15] Even if it is shown conclusively that Lukan pneumatology supports a doctrine of evidential tongues, it only validates one aspect of Pentecostal experience. But what the early Pentecostals experienced was not just a new surge of power for witness, but also a new sense of the nearness of the triune God, and it is *such* an experience that they claimed was evidenced by their speaking in tongues.

A Biblical Perspective of Spirit-Baptism

We will, therefore, have to begin with a broader and more integrated biblical understanding of Spirit-baptism than what the Lukan narrative provides. The biblical witness to this doctrine is quite broad and varied, as modern biblical scholarship has made clear. Matthew, for instance, sees baptism in the Spirit not as Jesus' giving the Spirit to his disciples (as in Luke and John) but as participation 'in Jesus' own inaugural empowerment by the Holy Spirit' at his baptism.

> The church has the Spirit...because, remaining with the church, Jesus baptizes with the Spirit through sharing his own baptism with the disciples of all ages. Jesus does not *give* the Spirit to the church but rather *receives* it *for* the church.[16]

---

14. See Donald L. Gelpi, S.J., 'Breath-Baptism in the Synoptics', in Cecil M. Robeck, Jr. (ed.), *Charismatic Experiences in History* (Peabody, MA: Hendricksen Press, 1985), pp. 15-43 (36).

15. So far, Menzies has not done much in the way of integrating Lukan and Pauline pneumatology.

16. McDonnell and Montague, *Christian Initiation*, p. 21.

Thus, for Matthew, believers are empowered through the abiding presence of Jesus who himself was baptized by the Spirit at his Jordan baptism. This motif comes through in Matthew in several ways, such as in the identification of Jesus as Immanuel, God with us (1.23); in Jesus' promise to the church of his abiding presence (28.20); and in the great commission where the implied authority needed to carry it out was given to Christ rather than delegated by him (28.18).[17]

For Mark, baptism in the Spirit is both empowerment by the Spirit as well as anointing to be a servant and the sacrifice for sin. Mark describes Jesus' passion as a 'baptism' (Mk 10.38-39).[18] Here again, the ethical dimension of the work of the Spirit is clearly in focus. Luke's pneumatology, on the other hand, needs a little more elaboration. A number of motifs appear to be quite widely accepted in current Lukan scholarship.[19] First, Luke seems to focus mainly on the charismatic work of the Spirit, particularly the 'gift of prophecy', a concept rooted in the Old Testament and inter-testamental literature. Luke's Gospel links the work of the Spirit mostly to certain forms of inspired speech (especially Luke 1 and 2). Second, Luke in the book of Acts views the work of Spirit largely in terms of empowering for witness or mission (1.8; 2.33-36, etc.). Third, Luke 'shows relatively little interest in the Spirit as the power of the spiritual, ethical and religious renewal of the individual'.[20] Yet, as Turner has argued (against Schweizer and Menzies),[21] the distinctive Lukan emphases do not preclude the soteriological and ethical elements.[22]

17. McDonnell and Montague, *Christian Initiation*, pp. 19-21.
18. McDonnell and Montague, *Christian Initiation*, pp. 10-11.
19. For an overview, see Max Turner, *The Holy Spirit and Spiritual Gifts* (Peabody, MA: Hendrickson, 1998), pp. 36-41.
20. Turner, *The Holy Spirit*, p. 39.
21. Eduard Schweizer, 'πνεῦμα πνευματικός', in G. Kittel (ed.), *Theological Dictionary of the New Testament*, VI (trans. Geoffrey W. Bromiley; 10 vols.; Grand Rapids: Eerdmans, 1968), pp. 404-415. For Menzies, see above n. 5.
22. Turner, *The Holy Spirit*, pp. 14-18, 33-35, 42-56. Both Eduard Schweizer and Robert Menzies think that Luke understands the gift of the Spirit as a *donum superadditum* or 'second blessing' given exclusively for empowerment for service and not for salvation. Such a view allows Menzies, a Pentecostal, to develop a doctrine of subsequence as a distinctively Lukan doctrine. Turner, however, has questioned this too narrow a view: '[T]he same gifts of the Spirit that fuel the mission (charismatic revelation, wisdom, prophecy, preaching and doxology) also

The Johannine writings, by contrast, appear to stand on the opposite end of the spectrum in relation to Luke. According to Turner, the focus is on Jesus as the giver of the Spirit after his death and resurrection (Jn 20.22-23).[23] The Spirit in turn reveals the significance of Jesus' death and resurrection. The eschatological gift of the Spirit is fulfilled in the Easter event (14.26; 15.26; 16.7). The charismatic gifts are not directly focused upon, although they are clearly implied (14.12).[24] For John, unlike Luke, the 'Spirit of prophecy' is 'the power to *reveal* God, especially in the word of Jesus' teaching and preaching'. John's focus is clearly on the revelatory role of the Spirit.[25]

It is in Paul's pneumatology that the soteriological and charismatic motifs achieve the highest integration. The soteriological motif can be seen in a number of ways. One is in terms of the strong Christocentric focus of Paul's pneumatology. The Spirit is called the 'Spirit of Christ', and this is to be understood in two ways: first, as the Spirit indwelling the believers who creates the character of Christ in them (Eph. 3.16, 17; Gal. 2.20; Rom. 8.9, 10), and secondly as the 'executive power' of Christ who relates to Christ in the same way as the Spirit is called the 'Spirit of Yahweh' in the Old Testament.[26] Further, the Spirit is also the Spirit of the new covenant. In Paul's contrast between the old covenant and new covenant in 2 Corinthians 3, it is clear that the decisive and differentiating element is the Spirit. 'The essence of the promised new covenant was that God would put his Spirit in men and women and thereby create in them a new heart and a new obedience.' Thus, receiving the Spirit is the same as being regenerated by the Spirit (Gal. 3.3-5, 14).[27] This new life is not thought of primarily as an individual reality but the result of being incorporated into Christ. In Christ, a new community or new creation is born (2 Cor. 5.17). This new creation is also an eschatological community in that the Spirit who indwells the com-

---

nurture, shape and purify the community, making it a messianic community of 'peace' conforming to the hopes for Israel's restoration' (p. 55).

23. Turner's limitation of the Spirit's activity in John's Gospel to after the resurrection (*The Holy Spirit*, p. 75), however, has been questioned by John Christopher Thomas, 'Max Turner's *The Holy Spirit and Spiritual Gifts: Then and Now* (Carlisle: Paternoster Press, 1996): An Appreciation and Critique', *Journal of Pentecostal Theology* 12 (1998), pp. 3-22 (16-17).

24. Turner, *The Holy Spirit*, pp. 56-62.

25. Turner, *The Holy Spirit*, pp. 57-89.

26. Turner, *The Holy Spirit*, pp. 122-23, 134.

27. Turner, *The Holy Spirit*, p. 117.

munity is only a 'downpayment' (2 Cor. 1.22; 5.5; Eph. 1.14).[28] In Paul, the charismatic dimension is closely linked to the soteriological: Paul sees in the ministry of the new covenant, the Spirit's role of removing the veil of ignorance, and the Spirit does this 'precisely by enabling the kind of wisdom or revelation that yields authentic understanding of the kerygma'.[29] Also, as the 'executive power' of Christ, the Spirit could be said to activate the gifts of Christ in the church (1 Cor. 12.7-11).

All these pneumatological motifs must be taken into consideration if we hope to develop an adequate theology of Spirit-baptism from the whole of Scripture. Above all, the comprehensive integration of Pauline pneumatology makes it imperative that the soteriological dimension which St Paul develops most fully becomes central to any discussion of Spirit-baptism. A Lukan theology of the Spirit, if we follow Schweizer and Menzies, does not provide an adequate basis for a Pentecostal theology. Turner has rightly noted, 'The fact is…that Paul's conception of the gift of the Spirit is simply *broader* than Luke's, *while nevertheless containing everything that Luke implies.*'[30] This means, among other things, that any doctrine about Spirit-baptism must deal ultimately with the relationship with the God who reveals himself in Jesus Christ through the illumination of the Spirit. Power is only the result of that revelational encounter with the triune God. Fee sums it up well when he says that for Paul, the Spirit is 'God's empowering *presence*'.[31] One cannot properly speak of the actualization of Spirit-baptism without introducing personal categories into the discussion, and it is in the context of personal encounter and intimacy that I hope to show that glossolalia functions as the most natural and pre-eminent sign.

A Theological Perspective of Spirit-Baptism

If the foregoing brief account of Spirit-baptism is correct, then it is possible to establish a theologically coherent relationship between Spirit-baptism (not just in the Lukan but also Pauline sense) and glossolalia. It is no longer a question of why Pentecostals should insist on tongues as a 'privileged marker', as Turner puts it, when there are in

28. Turner, *The Holy Spirit,* pp. 119-21.
29. Turner, *The Holy Spirit,* pp. 118-19.
30. Turner, *The Holy Spirit,* p. 154. Author's emphasis.
31. Fee, *God's Empowering Presence,* p. 8. My emphasis.

fact many other equally valid signs of Spirit-baptism.[32] Those who treat glossolalia as just one of the signs of the Spirit's presence have tended to operate on certain hermeneutical presuppositions, such as the authorial intention of Acts, or a collation of related texts.[33] Acts, of course, on such terms, could not support a doctrine of initial evidence. We need to look beyond the authorial intention to the Lukan theology of the Spirit and glossolalia, and even beyond Lukan theology to the total world view of the Scripture in which the coming of the Spirit and glossolalia form part of a larger, coherent pattern of the Christian life. In short, the way we should come to terms with the doctrine of Spirit-baptism and glossolalia should be the same as the way in which the church formulated its doctrine of the Trinity.[34] It is at this level of conceptualization that we uncover the rich symbolic meaning of glossolalia in relation to Spirit-baptism. The classic study of Herman Gunkel more than a century ago is a good case in point of such a broader approach. Gunkel came to the conclusion that glossolalia was 'the Spirit's most striking and characteristic activity'.[35] The special link between glossolalia and the Spirit, argued Gunkel, grew out of a *tradition* which sees the Spirit's presence in terms of spontaneous, dramatic and inexplicable actions so that the recipient of the experience of the Spirit is 'no longer agent' but 'passive'.[36] Gunkel's understanding of passivity in relation to the presence of the charismatic Spirit, perhaps needs to be further qualified. Passivity is not just a result of the charismatic activity of the Spirit, but, as we shall see, it has to do with a certain kind of personal relationship with God. The most appropriate context for understanding glossolalia, therefore, is not the *mantis* or ecstatic diviner,[37] but the contemplative. Still, the concept of passivity is crucial for understanding glossolalia as the 'most conspicuous' and 'most characteristic' sign of special kind of presence of the Spirit.

In recent years a number of Pentecostal scholars, using a similar theological approach, have helped the Pentecostal community to appreciate the deeper coherence between glossolalia and Spirit-baptism.

---

32. Turner, 'Tongues', p. 251.
33. E.g. Gordon Fee and Larry Hurtado. See nn. 3, 4 above.
34. See above, p. 29.
35. Hermann Gunkel, *The Influence of the Holy Spirit* (trans. Roy A. Harrisville and Philip A. Quanbeck II; Philadelphia: Fortress Press, 1979 [1888]), p. 30.
36. Gunkel, *Influence*, pp. 31-33.
37. Gunkel, *Influence*, pp. 31, 32.

The Catholic charismatic Simon Tugwell has developed what might be called a theology of speech.[38] He traces an early Christian tradition that links salvation to the opening of the mouth by the Holy Spirit.[39] Theologically, this is explained in terms of Rahner's 'primordial words'—words that link us to primal reality which do not need further explanations.[40] The revelation of God, the primal Reality, results in a human response in primordial words which are their own explanation for that theophany. Their very obscurity reveals the God who is unfathomable, or in the language of the Psalms, the One clothed in darkness (Ps. 18.11).Tugwell also shows the structural similarity between tongues and sacramental theology. The physical act of speaking in tongues is not only a pointer to but also embodies the spiritual reality: 'the primordial word is in the proper sense the presentation of the thing itself'.[41] What Pentecostals experienced in their initial Spirit-baptism is also something commonly reported in the conversion experience itself. One acts and yet feels that one could not have acted otherwise. The whole experience is characterized by an active passivity. The conversion experience of C.S. Lewis comes readily to mind here.[42]

If we are to locate this active passivity in Pentecostal experience theologically, we find its basis in the very trinitarian life of God itself. According to Barth, the majesty of God is seen in his *ad extra* work of sending his Son whose humility, subordination and obedience to the Father reveals precisely what the nature of the Godhead is like.[43] But this relationship is possible through the Holy Spirit, the bond of love between the Father and the Son. The same Spirit also binds the church to Christ its head and creates the same character of obedience, humility and self-surrender, the same 'active passivity' in the believers' relationship with God.[44] Glossolalia which is also an active passivity can be said to symbolize this basic relationship: we speak, yet it is a speech that comes from yieldedness and surrender to the will of God. Under-

---

38. Tugwell, 'The Speech-Giving Spirit', pp. 121-59.

39. Tugwell, 'The Speech-Giving Spirit', pp. 128-133.

40. Tugwell, 'The Speech-Giving Spirit', pp. 146-49.

41. Tugwell, 'The Speech-Giving Spirit', pp. 151-55 and Karl Rahner, *Theological Investigations*, III (London: Darton, Longman & Todd, 1967), p. 299.

42. C.S. Lewis, *Surprised by Joy* (London: Geoffrey Bles, 1955), p. 211.

43. Barth, *Church Dogmatics*, IV.1, p. 203. Barth here is not implying subordinationism, but the distinction in the Godhead based on the one *homoousion*.

44. Barth, *Church Dogmatics*, IV.1, pp. 209-10.

stood as such, glossolalia mirrors the most important characteristic of the divine life. It is a life of love and self-giving between the Father and the Son, in which the Father initiates and the Son yields in humble obedience by the power of the Spirit.

Another Pentecostal, Murray Dempster, understands glossolalia as a pointer to a reality of monumental proportion in the history of the church: the Pentecost event. The significance of tongues is ultimately linked to the significance of the Pentecost event itself.

> The Spirit's power to incorporate a group's participation in the creative remaking of language was a sign that portended the Spirit's power to initiate a group's participation in the creative remaking of history.[45]

Pentecost was the event that signalled the breaking down of the age-old racial divisions and the creation of a new spiritual order in which Jews and Gentiles, men and women, slaves and free participate as complete equals. Redemption is the creation of this new order of existence, and glossolalia as an inclusive experience symbolizes this new spiritual order.

Along lines similar to Tugwell's, Frank Macchia views tongues as a sacramental sign of Spirit-baptism. To call tongues a 'sacrament' implies an 'integral connection' between the sign and the thing signified.[46] In other words, if we examine the nature of tongues and the nature of Spirit-baptism we should be able to see some kind of deep coherence between the two. Macchia's explanation is well summed up in these words:

> Whether tongues were viewed as xenolalia or some form of transcendent glossolalia, their importance was the same. Here was a 'baptism' in the Spirit that allowed a weak human vessel to function as a veritable oracle of God. Though this is true of all prophetic speech, tongues as a cryptic language revealed the unfathomable depth and ultimate eschatological fulfillment of all prophetic speech, pointing to both the limits and the meaning of the language of faith. Without this 'glossolalic' understanding of Spirit baptism, there may not have been enough of a distinction between the Pentecostal and the Holiness understanding of the experience of the Spirit to warrant the founding of a separate movement.[47]

45. Murray Dempster, 'The Church's Moral Witness: A Study of Glossolalia in Luke's Theology of Acts', *Paraclete* 23.1 (Winter 1989), pp. 1-7 (3).

46. Frank D. Macchia, 'Groans Too Deep for Words: Towards a Theology of Tongues as Initial Evidence', *Asian Journal of Pentecostal Studies* 1.2 (1998), pp. 149-73. See especially p. 156.

47. Macchia, 'Groans Too Deep for Words', p. 167.

What these scholars have shown is that glossolalia functions as an appropriate, even a necessary, symbol of a spiritual reality and is not just an arbitrary sign. Using the 'cultural-linguistic' theory of doctrine developed by George Lindbeck, Macchia shows that glossolalia as a sacramental sign of Spirit-baptism makes perfect sense within the Pentecostal faith community.[48] The 'strangeness' of tongues corresponds to the 'strangeness' of the Pentecostal experience, while for Dempster the remaking of language symbolizes the remaking of history. There is a certain 'fittingness' between the sign and the thing signified. For Pentecostals, therefore, glossolalia was meant to signify a unique experience, something discontinuous with anything else that had been experienced before their Spirit-baptism. Only a unique sign was thought adequate to signify a unique reality. This claim to uniqueness of the Pentecostal reality must now be examined.

Contemporary theological interpretations of Spirit-baptism fall into two broad categories, the sacramental and non-sacramental. Basically, the non-sacramental interpretation sees Spirit-baptism as conversion-initiation and this view has been vigorously argued by James Dunn and followed by most evangelicals. A rare exception is Clark Pinnock, a Baptist, who follows the sacramental interpretation.[49] Those in the sacramental tradition (mostly Catholics and Orthodox) link Spirit-baptism to water baptism and confirmation. The Jesuit Francis A. Sullivan, however, adopts a non-sacramental interpretation. According to Sullivan, baptism in the Spirit is a fresh coming of the Spirit rather than an 'actualization' of grace already given.[50] But whether sacramentalist or non-sacramentalist, it is generally agreed that there is a Pentecostal dimension which is linked either to conversion-initiation or the sacrament of water baptism. Max Turner, who links Spirit-baptism to conversion, thinks that there is a greater 'degree' of intensity in the Pentecostal dimension of life, although he would dispute the Pentecostal claim to a different 'kind' of experience. The thrust of Turner's argument is that what the Pentecostals claim as unique is part of a reality that evangelicals also possess.[51] The way for evangelicals to become

48. Macchia, 'Groans Too Deep for Words', p. 168.
49. Clark H. Pinnock, *Flame of Love: A Theology of the Holy Spirit* (Downers Grove, IL: InterVarsity Press, 1996), pp. 124-29.
50. Francis A. Sullivan, *Charisms and Charismatic Renewal: A Biblical and Theological Study* (Ann Arbor, MI: Servant Books, 1982), pp. 69-70.
51. Turner, *The Holy Spirit*, esp. pp. 350, 356.

'charismatics' is only a matter of 'redirect[ing] their emphases and expectations'.[52] The charismatic dimension refers to the 'renewing, ongoing, and extending experiences and appropriations of the gift of the Spirit given to all Christians in conversion-initiation'.[53] Turner's understanding reflects a tendency of evangelicals to narrow the experiential gap between evangelicals and Pentecostals. This is partly due to the fact that evangelicals already see conversion as an experiential reality, but a reality which needs further intensification without making it distinct from Spirit-baptism.[54] I shall return to Turner's point later. The sacramentalists, on the other hand, see Spirit-baptism as the 'actualization' of a reality within a unified initiation ritual which includes water baptism and confirmation.[55] The two rites are distinct because they reveal or convey two distinct experiential realities in conversion-initiation. It is for this reason that perhaps a sacramental view of Spirit-baptism may be more useful in clarifying the nature of the Pentecostal reality. I shall take this up again in Chapter 3.

But what is it about this reality which makes Pentecostal-charismatics claim that their experience is different from other Christians? I have noted previously that 'revelation' rather than power is the more basic category for understanding the nature of baptism in the Spirit. The revelation is that of God in the personal presence of Jesus Christ. McDonnell has noted that when Pentecostals speak of God's presence, they are referring to 'a primary closeness to Jesus to the point of touching from within'.[56] David A. Dorman describes it as 'a personal disclosure of God particularly as to His immediacy' resulting in 'a qualitatively different life lived in the light...of that striking sense of the nearness of God'.[57] Similarly, Macchia sees the Spirit's work of revelation as a 'theophany' which highlights its irruptive and invasive nature.[58] The revelation resulted in a new relationship with God through

---

52. Turner, *The Holy Spirit*, p. 357.

53. Turner, *The Holy Spirit*, p. 164.

54. Cf. Turner, 'Tongues', p. 251.

55. McDonnell and Montague, *Christian Initiation*, pp. 89, 97.

56. Kilian McDonnell, 'The Function of Tongues in Pentecostalism', *One in Christ* 19.4 (1983), pp. 332-54 (340).

57. David A. Dorman, 'The Purpose of Empowerment in the Christian Life', *Pneuma* 7.2 (Fall 1985), pp. 147-65 (147-48).

58. Theophany as a theological term refers to a more focused form of divine revelation and is therefore a more appropriate description of the Pentecostal reality than the broader term revelation.

the Spirit. There is a deep awareness of the nearness of God and a holy familiarity. Along with it, the extraordinary charisms are activated. The charisms, therefore, must always be interpreted in the context of the presence of God. This is the way in which the Pentecostal *locus classicus*, Acts 1.8 should be understood. Acts 1.8 is not just about being empowered to witness as a result of being baptized in the Spirit; it is first and foremost about *being* witnesses, about lives being transformed.[59] More specifically, it is lives transformed by the power of the resurrection through union with Christ. In sharing Christ's resurrected life, believers are released from the fear of death into a self-transcending freedom which enables them to place themselves at God's complete disposal.[60] In such a state the charisms become truly edifying to the body of Christ rather than the means of self-aggrandisement.

Extraordinary charisms, from one perspective, could be regarded as a sign of highly focused personal activity. They belong to the very nature of what it means to be a person. Of all creatures, only personal beings are capable of springing surprises because only they are truly free. Macchia sums it up well when he says, 'The element of spontaneity and wonder in such theophanic encounters with God have always been the heart-throb of Pentecostal spirituality and attraction to tongues.'[61] Yet, these surprises that interrupt the ordinary flow of life, making us deeply aware that life consists of more than just calculated predictability, are themselves part of the fabric of life. The Pentecostal reality is an inextricable part of ordinary Christian living, yet at the same time it is discontinuous with it. The Christian life as the Pentecostal sees it consists essentially of the interplay of the extraordinary and the ordinary. Such a view is analogous to a point in traditional dogmatics which distinguishes between providence and miracles, or, if we may draw an analogy from modern physics, between the predictability of 'everyday physics' and the unpredictability of chaos theory.[62] This is not to suggest that extraordinary charismatic experiences are always to be understood in terms of direct divine interventions, but that they represent a

59. Dorman, 'Purpose of Empowerment', p. 150.

60. Cf. Jean-Jacques Suurmond, 'The Meaning and Purpose of Spirit-Baptism and the Charisms', in Jan A.B. Jongeneel (ed.), *Experiences of the Spirit* (Frankfurt Am Main: Peter Lang, 1991), pp. 35-62.

61. Suurmond, 'The Meaning and Purpose of Spirit-Baptism', p. 55.

62. Cf. John Polkinghorne, *Serious Talk: Science and Religion in Dialogue* (London: SCM Press, 1996), pp. 76-90.

different, heightened level of personal awareness.[63] Sometimes Pentecostals express the discontinuous dimension of their experience with their 'vocabulary of "more"'. As one Swedish Pentecostal put it,

> God...made it very clear that there was more than forgiveness and sonship to be received from him. I not only understand there *was* more for me, but felt that there *must* be more for me, or otherwise my Christian life would be a failure.[64]

The logic of the Pentecostal claim, therefore, is similar to the logic of play. (I will take this up in the last chapter.) The very nature of play is that it requires the demarcation of specific times for play. There is a beginning and end of play, and within the period called play-time, the players step out of the ordinary world into a different world. They are involved in what would be described in literary circles as 'the willing suspension of unbelief'. For many Christians entering the Pentecostal world is like entering the world of play. The transition is just as definite as to be described as a major paradigm shift, a crossing of the threshold, a 'breakthrough in communication'.[65] In this transition glossolalia has a peculiar function which helps to explain why classical Pentecostals came to regard it as 'the initial evidence'. It is the means which enables the speaker to open up to a new spiritual dimension. Cardinal Suenens made this interesting observation about tongues:

> If St. Paul treats this gift as the least of all...might this not be because it is, in a sense, a way that leads to the other gifts, a small doorway as it were, which can only be entered by stooping...? The gift of tongues, which has nothing to do with the intellect, makes a breach in the 'reserve' we assume as a system of defense. It helps us cross a threshold and, in doing so, attain a new freedom in our surrender to God.[66]

Whether glossolalia is actually the least of the gifts is a moot point, but it is certainly far more than just the intensification of a pre-existing reality, as many evangelicals insist. This evangelical explanation simply does not ring true to this quintessential Pentecostal experience.

---

63. Peter Hocken, 'The Significance and Potential of Pentecostalism', in *New Heaven? New Earth?* (Springfield, IL: Templegate Publishers, 1976), pp. 15-67 (23).

64. Cited by McDonnell, 'Function of Tongues', p. 342.

65. Tugwell, 'The Speech-Giving Spirit', p. 139.

66. Léon Joseph Suenens, *A New Pentecost?* (trans. Francis Martin; New York: Seabury Press, 1975), p. 102.

The evangelical view has serious repercussions for our understanding of spiritual progress. I shall return to this point later.

A Cultural-Linguistic Perspective of Spirit-Baptism

Within the Pentecostal 'cultural-linguistic' community Pentecostals are able to make sense of the fact that glosssolalia 'fits' their experience of Spirit-baptism. But the challenge has come from outside the Pentecostal community: Is it right, then, to call tongues '*the* initial physical evidence'? The issue, therefore, must be pressed further. Given the theological significance of tongues for the Pentecostal community, can that explanation be justified before the larger Christian community?[67] I have suggested elsewhere that it is justifiable to regard glossolalia as initial evidence when the experience to which it refers is characterized by receptivity.[68] Pentecostals see evidential tongues as God's action to which the believer simply yields. This strong sense of God's action is parallel to the way that sacraments are traditionally perceived: they are God's action in human acts.[69] What Pentecostals experience in glossolalia is nothing more or less than what has always been seen as something utterly basic and essential to prayer itself. Prayer is by nature never a human initiative but a receptive response to the God who first spoke the word to us. Prayer, as Hans Urs von Balthasar puts it, 'is communication, in which God's word has the initiative and we...are simply listeners'.[70] Glossolalia simply encapsulates this truth concerning the divine-human interchange most concretely. Tongues are the primordial words (to use Rahner's term) that arise spontaneously in response to the invasive coming of the primal Reality to the believers which Pentecostals identify as a Spirit-baptism. The experience of Spirit-baptism entails a paradigm shift of such proportion that one spontaneously responds in tongues, much in the same way as we are accustomed to associating tears with sadness.[71] The presence of tears signifies

---

67. This is a valid point that Tan May Ling makes in her response to Macchia's essay, 'A Response to Frank Macchia's "Groans Too Deep for Words: Towards A Theology of Tongues as Initial Evidence"', *Asian Journal of Pentecostal Studies* 1.2 (1998), pp. 175-83 (182).

68. Simon Chan, 'The Language Game of Glossolalia', pp. 87-88.

69. Congar, *I Believe*, II, p. 175, citing Tugwell, 'The Speech-Giving Spirit', p. 151.

70. Hans Urs von Balthasar, *On Prayer* (London: SPCK, 1961), p. 12.

71. See Congar, *I Believe*, II, p. 173; Simon Tugwell, *Did you Receive the*

in a unique way the reality of sadness. Of course, tears could signify other realities (such as joy) and sadness could be evidenced by other signs (like rage). But between tears and sadness, there is a connaturality such that one simply recognizes, by a primal act of recognition,[72] the one in the presence of the other. The difficulty with a term like 'evidence' is that it can all too easily be misunderstood as indicating a causal connection, as seen, for example, in such misplaced questions as, must one speak in tongues in order to be filled with the Spirit? If one does not speak in tongues does it mean that one is not Spirit-filled? One does not ask: must one cry in order to be sad? Glossolalia does not have the status of proof. Perhaps a better term to describe the connection between glossolalia and Spirit-baptism is concomitant. Glossolalia is not just one of the concomitants of being Spirit-filled, but is the most natural and regular concomitant of Spirit-filling involving an invasive or irruptive manifestation of the Spirit in which one's relationship to Jesus Christ is radically and significantly altered. When one experiences the coming of the Spirit in such a manner, the most natural and spontaneous response is glossolalia. Like the gift of tears, glossolalia is not something to be sought but something to be received freely as a gift.[73]

This aspect of the Pentecostal-charismatic experience is in fact very similar to the 'passive' phases of contemplative prayer in the Christian mystical tradition. In Teresa of Avila prayer progresses from the active (ascetical) phase to the passive phase, from 'acquired' contemplation to 'infused' contemplation. The transition from ascetical prayer to the prayer of quiet is achieved by the 'prayer of recollection'[74] which Rowan Williams has vividly described as

> the state in which the inner gaze of the soul is becoming more and more steadily fixed on God's self-giving, and that steady regard finds expression in simple patterns of words; as this deepens and simplifies, God's activity engages us with greater completeness, and our deepest 'mental' activities are reduced to silence...[75]

Spirit? (London: Darton, Longman & Todd, 1972), p. 63.

72. It is similar to what Michael Polanyi calls 'tacit knowing'. See *The Tacit Dimension* (Gloucester, MA: Peter Smith, 1983), pp. 3-25.

73. Teresa of Avila, 'The Interior Castle', in *idem, The Collected Works of St Teresa of Avila*, II (trans. Kieran Kavanaugh and Otilio Rogriguez; Washington, DC: ICS Publications, 1980), pp. 263-452 (394-95).

74. Teresa of Avila, 'The Interior Castle', pp. 327-34.

75. Rowan Williams, *Teresa of Avila* (Harrisburg, PA: Moorehouse Publishing, 1991), pp. 125-26.

The passive phase begins at the fourth 'mansion' which Teresa calls the prayer of quiet.[76] Here is the beginning of 'supernatural experiences' given by God apart from any effort on our part.[77] The preceding three 'mansions' of prayer engage the soul actively, whereas from the fourth level, the soul becomes increasingly receptive. Along with progression from active to passive prayer, the soul also experiences progression of joy. In the ascetical phases where discursive prayer and meditation are the main forms of prayer, the soul experiences 'consolations'. Consolations are the effects of ascetical prayers, although Teresa is quick to add that even here 'God does have a hand in them'.[78] But in the fourth mansion the soul receives 'spiritual delight' from God. This spiritual delight does not come from our actively seeking it, although the ascetical phases of prayer prepared the way for it. Teresa uses the picture of two troughs to illustrate the difference between the active and passive phases of prayer. In the active phase, the trough receives its water 'through many aqueducts and the use of much ingenuity', that is to say, through spiritual exercises such as meditation. But in the second phase, water is poured directly from God overflowing the trough and filling the soul with 'spiritual delight'.

> [God] produces this delight with the greatest peace and quiet and sweetness in the very interior part of ourselves...; this water overflows through all the dwelling places and faculties until reaching the body. That is why I said that it begins in God and ends in ourselves. For...the whole exterior man enjoys this spiritual delight and sweetness.[79]

In an autobiographical exposition of the soul's progress in prayer, Teresa covers basically the same ground as the 'Interior Castle' but speaks instead of four degrees of prayer: discursive meditation, prayer of recollection and quiet, prayer of the sleep of the faculties, and prayer of union.[80] The third degree is particularly interesting. At this point the faculties are 'asleep' so that 'the faculties neither fail entirely to function nor understand how they function'. In such a state the soul experiences the most indescribable delight:

76. Teresa of Avila, 'The Interior Castle', p. 323.
77. Teresa of Avila, 'The Interior Castle', p. 316.
78. Teresa of Avila, 'The Interior Castle', pp. 317-18.
79. Teresa of Avila, 'The Interior Castle', p. 324.
80. Teresa of Avila, 'The Book of her Life', in *idem*, *The Collected Works of St Teresa of Avila*, I, pp. 78-152.

I don't know any other terms for describing it or how to explain it. Nor does the soul then know what to do because it doesn't know whether to speak or to be silent, whether to laugh or to weep. This prayer is a glorious foolishness, a heavenly madness where the true wisdom is learned; and it is for the soul a most delightful way of enjoying.[81]

At this point Teresa describes the response of the soul as follows:

What is the soul like when it is in this state! It would want to be *all tongues* so as to praise the Lord. It speaks folly in a thousand holy ways, even trying to find means of pleasing the one who thus possessed it.[82]

Teresa's characterization of this phase of prayer in which joy becomes so overwhelming that the soul could only respond with 'all tongues' and 'heavenly madness' bears the closest resemblance to the Pentecostal experience of Spirit-baptism accompanied by glossolalia. One early Pentecostal described Spirit-baptism as the occasion when the 'yielded human vessel is controlled entirely by the divine Spirit— hence unlimited and unrestrained' and 'when by the Spirit Himself, using their yielded, enraptured faculties, they [the believers in Acts 2] began to magnify God...in divers languages'.[83] I am not suggesting that every case of evidential tongues coincides exactly with Teresa's passive prayers. The coincidence is more structural than material. It is likely that in most cases glossolalia represents the lower levels of passive prayer, or the transition from active to passive prayer (although the level of intimacy represented by glossolalia may depend very much on the maturity of the believer prior to his or her experiencing glossolalia).

The main difference between the Pentecostal and the mystic is that the former's receptivity is signalled predominantly by glossolalia while the latter's is signalled by a wider variety of responses, including silence and some form of ecstatic utterances of praise. But the difference may be due to the more developed theology of prayer in the mystical tradition which enables the mystic to reflect on his or her experience with greater precision. It is also possible that as Pentecostal-charismatics continue to reflect on their experience of tongues, they will discover more areas of experience in the mystical tradition with which they could readily identify. For example, in the study by the Doctrine

81. Teresa of Avila, 'Life', 16.1.

82. Teresa of Avila, 'Life', 16.4. Italics mine.

83. Cited by Gary B. McGee, 'Popular Expositions of Initial Evidence', in *idem*, (ed.), *Initial Evidence*, p. 128.

Commission of the General Synod of the Church of England on the Holy Spirit in 1989, interviews with Anglican charismatics indicated many areas of convergence. Speaking in tongues was often 'a repetitive and formalised sound'—much like the Jesus Prayer; some saw their experience of silence as the 'point' or 'end' of tongues; many experienced tongues as 'ceding to the Spirit', an act of 'surrender' etc.[84]

Glossolalia and silence are functionally equivalent, as Richard Baer has pointed out.[85] Both symbolize a response from the depth of the human spirit to the reality of God felt as an immediate presence. Such a response reveals the limits of human rationality and the need to transcend it. Their difference may be regarded as different sub-dialects within the same language game. Or, if we use Lindbeck's categories, we may say that each is operating according to its own cultural-linguistic 'grammar'.[86] Within the Catholic tradition, silence and ecstatic speech are the regulative grammar for 'evidencing' this focused presence of God, while in the Pentecostal community it is glossolalia. Each community develops its own distinguishing mark of recognition. Glossolalia, as Kilian McDonnell has pointed out, is a 'commitment act' signalling a person's initiation into the Pentecostal community.[87] This does not mean that glossolalia is merely a socio-cultural marker, a prearranged requirement to initiate one into the Pentecostal faith community. It is first a theological marker whose truth can be tested against certain spiritual experiences which Pentecostals share with other segments of the Christian community.[88] Thus by locating glossolalia within

84. *We Believe in the Holy Spirit: A Report by the Doctrine Commission of the General Synod of the Church of England* (London: Church House Publishing, 1993), pp. 26, 27. Hereafter referred to as the Doctrine Commission.

85. Richard A. Baer, Jr. 'Quaker Silence, Catholic Liturgy, and Pentecostal Glossolalia—Some Functional Similarities', in Russell P. Spittler (ed.), *Perspectives on the New Pentecostalism* (Grand Rapids: Baker Book House, 1976), pp. 152-54.

86. The need to understand glossolalia within its own cultural-linguistic context is shown in a recent article by Shuman, 'Toward a Cultural-Linguistic Account', pp. 207-223.

87. McDonnell, 'Function of Tongues', p. 337.

88. What I am suggesting here is broadly similar to Amos Yong's attempt to establish the truth of glossolalia based on criteria derived from the theory of religious symbolism developed by Robert C. Neville. These criteria are not just about whether glossolalia corresponds to anything 'out there' (the correspondence criterion of truth). The coherence and pragmatic criteria must also be included. Coherence refers to the interpretation of glossolalia as a theological symbol in

the larger context of the mystical tradition, it makes perfectly good sense to say that glossolalia is the initial evidence or concomitant of Spirit-baptism, in much the same way as silence or some other glossolalia-like response signifies the soul's surrender to God in passive prayer. This is as far as Pentecostal apologetics could go. To look for a more 'objective' defence of glossolalia implies that there is a larger context beyond Christianity against which the latter must be judged.[89] I do not think this is what our non-Pentecostal brethren expected of us. Glossolalia as initial evidence is very much an issue within the household of faith.

Spirit-Baptism as Spirituality

Ultimately, if the distinctive Pentecostal doctrine of glossolalia is to commend itself, it must be shown to entail a more adequate spirituality compared with other explanations of it.[90] How do evidential tongues function as part of a coherent Pentecostal way of life? I approach this question by contrasting the ways in which evangelicals and Pentecostals would have located tongues in their respective spiritual frameworks. Suppose someone had an experience of glossolalia. The counsel

relation to a network of other theological symbols as well as what divine reality glossolalia intends to disclose, while the pragmatic criterion refers to how people's practices are transformed by the symbol. (Amos Yong, ' "Tongues of Fire" in the Pentecostal Imagination: The Truth of Glossolalia in the Light of R.C. Neville's Theory of Religious Symbolism', *Journal of Pentecostal Theology* 12 [1998], pp. 39-65).

89. It should be noted that Lindbeck's cultural-linguistic theory of doctrine has been criticized for its tendency to focus purely on the intrasystemic aspect of the doctrine and its refusal to address the question of Christianity's truth-claims. See Alister E. McGrath, *The Genesis of Doctrine* (Oxford: Basil Blackwell, 1990), pp. 20-34. I do not think, however, that the problem is inherent to the cultural-linguistic theory itself. In other words, Lindbeck's theory does not necessarily exclude the cognitive or external referents of Christian discourse. But what it does show is that the *justification* of Christian truth-claims can only be made from within the Christian interpretive community. In our case, we are concerned only with the justification of glossolalia in the Pentecostal community, which could be understood as a sub-cultural-linguistic system within the larger Christian community. The justification of glossolalia as initial evidence is possible by showing that it fits the grammar of the larger community.

90. This form of vindication of glossolalia corresponds to Yong's pragmatic criterion of truth, ' "Tongues of Fire" in the Pentecostal Imagination', p. 49.

given by the evangelical would probably go like this: 'You have just received one of those "refreshings" that God occasionally sends on us. Remember the refreshing he gives Bunyan's Christian on the Delectable Mountain? Thank God for the gift of tongues, but don't confine yourself to it, seek the other gifts as well, especially those that will build up the church.' The Pentecostal, on the other hand, would probably counsel thus: 'Your experience indicates that God intends to lead you into a deeper walk with him. But this is only the beginning. If you will use the gift faithfully as part of your prayer life, you will find it to be an avenue of further deepening your walk with God. There will be other surprises as you go along, like a new boldness to share your faith, or the discovery of an ability to minister to others which you never thought was possible. But don't be preoccupied with the gifts. Continue to cultivate your walk with God using the avenue that he has opened for you.'

I think it is the Pentecostal rather than evangelical explanation that rings truer to what the new charismatic had experienced. Almost certainly, the majority of the church's mystics would have received the Pentecostal explanation quite sympathetically. They would have seen in glossolalia echoes of their own experience in infused contemplation. This may explain why Catholic charismatics have been far less averse to the initial evidence doctrine than the evangelicals.[91] The evangelical understanding will lead to one of two possibilities. New charismatics will come to accept the evangelical explanation, tone down their enthusiasm and after a few weeks or months return to basically where they were before. They would probably have noticed that they were none the better or worse for the experience. We see this among Christians who would declare that they had spoken in tongues once, but thought nothing much of it. Or, the new charismatic will accept the evangelical explanation in principle but then finds it increasingly difficult to reconcile the explanation with his or her own increasingly frequent 'refreshings'. What is likely to happen next is that he or she will become more and more enamoured of the charisms particularly of the more spectacular kind and will come to see them as definitive of what it means to be a

---

91. The similarity between tongues and various manifestations associated with infused contemplation has been noted by many Catholic authors like J. Massingberd Ford, Louis Bouyer, Simon Tugwell and others. See Peter Hocken, 'Pentecostals on Paper II: Baptism in the Spirit and Speaking in Tongues', *The Clergy Review* 60 (1975), pp. 161-83.

charismatic. This is what we are seeing among the 'Third Wavers'.

If glossolalia is to be understood as the initial evidence (or the concomitant) of Spirit-baptism, it must be linked to something that is far larger than traditional Pentecostal conceptualizations of it (such as empowering for mission). It must be shown to constitute an essential part of a coherent schema of spiritual development in which one experiences growing intimacy with God and holiness of life. In short, without this final correlation between glossolalia and holiness, I doubt if the Pentecostal reality could be sustainable.

To do this, we need first to recall the biblical witness which links power (charisms) and holiness. The overall thrust of New Testament pneumatology views charismatic power within the larger context of an ethical community in covenant relationship with God. This is especially true for Paul and even for Luke. This link between power and holiness is especially pronounced in Matthew.[92] The Matthean pneumatology which links power with the presence of Jesus implies a certain theology of miracles: that the ensuing power of being filled with the Spirit must not be divorced from a life lived in intimate relationship with God. Miracles apart from holiness are in fact soul-destroying. '[T]he Christian charismatic,' notes Montague, 'is authenticated by a life of personal holiness.'[93] This is the reason for the sombre warning of Mt. 7.21-23:

> Not everyone who says to me 'Lord, Lord,' will enter the kingdom of heaven, but only he who does the will of my Father who is in heaven. Many will say to me on that day, 'Lord, Lord, did we not prophesy in your name, and in your name drive out demons and perform many miracles?' Then I will tell them plainly, 'I never knew you. Away from me, you evil-doers!'

This is a message that modern charismatics obsessed with signs and wonders must take special note of. While it is possible for charisms to be exercised apart from holiness, both Scripture and the Christian tradition have been consistently opposed to such a practice. The Christian tradition has quite early developed a theology of miracles to address this issue. The desert fathers understood the lure of spiritual power, precisely because their deep cultivation of the spiritual life had led them

92. As noted above by McDonnell and Montague, *Christian Initiation*, p. 21.
93. George T. Montague, *The Holy Spirit: Growth of a Biblical Tradition* (Peabody, MA: Hendrickson Press, 1976), p. 309.

to have direct contact with it. John Cassian in the fourth century distinguished three kinds of miracles: those performed by men of holiness; those performed for the sake of the church or because of the faith of those who brought their sick even though the persons through whom the miracles were performed may be sinners; and those inspired by demons.[94] Thomas Aquinas (1225–1274) too distinguishes two types of 'true miracles' wrought by the power of God corresponding to Cassian's first two types. One type is 'in proof of a person's holiness' and the other is 'for the confirmation of truth declared'. According to Aquinas, even wicked people can sometimes perform the second kind of miracles.

> Miracles are always true witnesses to the purpose for which they are wrought. Hence wicked men who teach a false doctrine never work true miracles in confirmation of their teaching, although sometimes they may do so in praise of Christ's name which they invoke, and by the power of the sacraments which they administer. If they teach a true doctrine, sometimes they work true miracles as confirming their teaching, but not as an attestation of holiness.[95]

The fact that miracles can occur apart from sanctity must not detract us from seeing miracles overflowing from a life of holiness as the norm. There is no reason for one to be content with an unsanctified Pentecostalism even if one's ministry remains effective. It is quite likely, however, that when one performs a miracle of the first kind, that is, as an outcome of one's holiness, he or she is not going to pay too much attention to the miraculous per se. Cassian noted that this was the way the holy desert fathers treated miracles.

> We see...that the working of signs was never made much of by our fathers. On the contrary, although they possessed this by the grace of the Holy Spirit, they never wanted to exercise it unless perchance an extreme and unavoidable necessity forced them.[96]

Cassian then went on to cite the examples of Abba Macarius and Abba Abraham who performed healings with great reluctance.[97] We see a modern example of this attitude in Sadhu Sundar Singh. Even though

---

94. John Cassian, *The Conferences* (trans. Boniface Ramsey O.P.; New York: Paulist Press, 1997), 15.1.

95. Thomas Aquinas, *Summa Theologica* (60 vols.; New York: Blackfriars, 1964–) Pt. II.2, Q. 178.2.

96. Cassian, *Conferences*, 15.2.

97. Cassian, *Conferences*, 15.3-5.

his ministry was accompanied by very spectacular miracles, he did not pay much attention to them, much less hold seminars on 'how to have signs and wonders accompanying your ministry'. When he found out that the healings that took place through his prayers were causing people to look upon him as a wonder-worker and he could not convince them to believe that it was Christ who healed, Sundar Singh decided to stop exercising the gift, as 'it would encourage superstition and distract from the gospel'.[98] The overall biblical perspective of Spirit-baptism, which places the charismatic dimension within a soteriological or ethical context, needs to be reinforced if present-day Pentecostals hope to move on to a mature and sustainable spirituality.

The goal is to cultivate a praxis of supernatural charisms that moves us from a fixation on the spectacular to a ministry that recognizes the conjunction of miracles and sanctity. But what is the nature of this sanctified life? Here again, the desert fathers are most helpful. They believed that it is the virtue of humility that will ensure the sane and safe exercise of spiritual gifts.

> Humility...is the teacher of all the virtues; it is the most firm foundation of the heavenly edifice; it is the Savior's own magnificent gift. For a person may perform without danger of pride all the miracles that Christ worked if he strains after the meek Lord not because of his exalted signs but because of his patience and humility. But a person who itches to command unclean spirits, to bestow the gift of health on the sick, or to show some wondrous sign to the people is far from Christ even though he invokes the name of Christ in his displays, because by reason of his proud mind he does not follow the Teacher of humility.[99]

Without humility those who perform miracles will quickly draw attention to themselves and misuse the gifts that are meant to bless others.[100] Humility is a kind of self-forgetfulness. Humility, according to C.S. Lewis, is like sleep: if one is truly asleep one does not know it; to know oneself to be asleep is to be half awake. The piece of wisdom from the desert fathers is coming to be better appreciated by some

---

98. A.J. Appasamy, *Sundar Singh: A Biography* (Madras: The Christian Literature Society, 1990 [1958]), pp. 98-99. Cf. Friedrich Heiler, *The Gospel of Sadhu Sundar Singh* (trans. Olive Wyon; New Delhi: ISPCK, 1989), pp. 182-85. Heiler's assessment of the sadhu's attittude towards miracles is that it is 'more spiritual than many Christian saints, whether ancient or modern' (p. 184).

99. Cassian, *Conferences*, 15.7.

100. Cassian, *Conferences*, 15.7.

modern-day Pentecostals. In an insightful essay using the model of developmental psychology propounded by James E. Loder, Jean-Jacques Suurmond explores the relationship between the charisms and Spirit-baptism. According to Suurmond, Spirit-baptism could be seen as 'the experience of the resurrection life of Christ, which liberates his followers again and again from the fear of death: thus enabling a life of self-giving love through the charisms'.[101] Charisms, then, are not something external to ourselves, a sort of impersonal tool we can skilfully manipulate and use to do the work of the kingdom of God. They are the extension of the one charism: the gift (charisma) of eternal life in Christ (Rom. 6.23). The nature of the resurrection life is that it grows out of death to self and turns us from self-preoccupation towards selfless service to others. '"Cleansed" from our neurotic self-limitation, our body rises...as an "instrument of righteousness" in a heroic gift which builds up (or edifies) others.'[102] What Suurmond says using the language of theology and psychology, the desert fathers had anticipated using the direct language of Scripture and traditional virtue ethics.

It is in this connection that we can understand why the first ten years represent the heart of Pentecostalism. During the first ten years, according to Edith Blumhofer, most Pentecostals believed that Spirit-baptism was preceded by entire sanctification.[103] This ensures that the empowering experience does not hang loose from the larger framework of Christian existence. Sanctification ensures that Pentecostal affections remain basically 'gracious' (yet powerful) affections, to use Jonathan Edwards's terminology. The early years also saw holiness expressed in strong social concerns. Even in Latin America today, where historically the Pentecostal tradition developed quite independently of its North American counterpart, we find a Pentecostalism that fulfils the role of what Hauerwas calls a 'contrast community'. Brazilian Pentecostalism in particular has been noted for its vibrant social engagement. Cheryl

101. Jean-Jacques Suurmond, 'The Meaning and Purpose of Spirit-Baptism and the Charisms', in Jongeneel, *Experiences of the Spirit*, p. 35.

102. Suurmond, 'Meaning and Purpose', p. 45.

103. Edith L. Blumhofer, 'Purity and Preparation: A Study in the Pentecostal Perfectionist Heritage', in Stanley M. Burgess (ed.), *Reaching Beyond: Chapters in the History of Perfectionism* (Peabody, MA: Hendricksen Press, 1986), pp. 270-79. See also Walter Hollenweger, *The Pentecostals* (Peabody, MA: Hendricksen Press, 1988), pp. 24-26.

Johns describes it as 'a liberating movement of the masses'.[104] But 1910 was the watershed year. It marked the beginning of the fragmentation of Pentecostal spirituality when William H. Durham repudiated the Wesleyan-Holiness view of a three-stage view of the spiritual life (that is, conversion, entire sanctification and Spirit-baptism) and advocated a two-stage development—minus entire sanctification. Entire sanctification was no longer a prerequisite for Spirit-baptism. Rather, Durham accepted the Reformed view that righteousness was imputed followed by progressive sanctification. According to Durham, it is 'the living faith that justifies a man, brings him into Christ, the Sanctifier, in Whom he is complete, not with regard to sanctification only, but everything else that pertains to his salvation'.[105] Justification by faith becomes the catch-all reality which includes sanctification and 'everything else that pertains to...salvation'. The result was to turn sanctification into an indistinct part of the salvation complex. One could get filled with the Spirit apart from any *discernible* sanctification. The five-fold gospel (Jesus as Saviour, Sanctifier, Baptizer, Healer and Coming King) became the four-fold gospel, dropping 'Sanctifier'.[106] I am not suggesting that we should re-establish the doctrine of entire sanctification as a second work of grace any more than we should interpret Spirit-baptism as a second work of grace. But a failure to understand Spirit-baptism in relation to sanctification has resulted in power being divorced from holiness. The fag-end of this theological shift can now be seen in travesties of Christianity among the independent charismatic preachers and television evangelists.

The early Pentecostals' pneumatology was far more wholesome than their modern counterparts'. First, it was essentially Christocentric rather than pneumatocentric. The five-fold gospel is about *Jesus* as Saviour etc. not about the Spirit. This ensured that Christ and not power was the main focus of the Pentecostal message. As one early Pentecostal put it,

> When we get the baptism with the Holy Spirit, we have something to tell, and it is that the blood of Jesus Christ cleanseth from all sin. The baptism with the Holy Ghost gives us power to testify to a risen, resur-

104. Bridges-Johns, *Pentecostal Formation*, p. 77.

105. Cited by Blumhofer, 'Purity and Preparation', pp. 275-76. The 'finished work' controversy, as it came to be called, split the early Pentecostal movement and is far from being over (see Hollenweger, *The Pentecostals*, p. 25).

106. Hollenweger, *The Pentecostals*, pp. 185-87.

rected Savior. Our affections are in Jesus Christ, the Lamb of God that takes away the sin of the world.[107]

Second, the five-fold gospel ensured a healthy integration between holiness and power. Land has observed that '[t]hroughout the literature of the early revival there is this explicit correlation of the righteousness, holiness and power of God and the righteousness, love and power of the believer'.[108] Power without the prerequisite of sanctity is ultimately destructive, especially if it is spiritual power. In integrating power and holiness the early Pentecostals had in fact adopted a position not very different from that found in the Catholic spiritual tradition where true miracles are normatively associated with sainthood, as noted above in Thomas Aquinas and the desert fathers. They may not have developed a fully-fledged Thomistic theology of miracles, but their five-fold gospel certainly has the potential of becoming one.

This point needs a little elaboration. Gordon Fee has suggested that we see charismatic operations as one component in the salvation complex.[109] To follow through Fee's suggestion, we need to inquire into the precise nature of the relationship between the gifts and the Christian life. The Thomistic conjunction of miracles and sainthood offers a theological basis for understanding the relationship. The miraculous is grace freely given (*gratia data gratis*), but at the same time it occurs more freely in a life that is in deep communion with God. Jesus is the supreme model of such a life. As man he was empowered by the Spirit in his mission, yet unlike us he was a sinless man, in perfect communion with God, wholly open to the will of God and able to discern clearly God's will in a given situation. The Johannine account of his communion with the Father seems to bear this out. Jesus is completely accessible to the Father and the Father to him. Before the tomb of Lazarus he declares: 'Father, I thank you that you have heard me. I knew that you always hear me' (Jn 11.41).[110] Is it possible that because of his complete openness to God, he knows when to heal and when not, and this is the basis for his outstanding miracles and hundred per cent

---

107. Quoted by Land, *Pentecostal Spirituality*, p. 129.

108. Land, *Pentecostal Spirituality*, p. 129.

109. Gordon Fee, 'Baptism in the Holy Spirit: The Issue of Separability and Subsequence', *Pneuma* 7.2 (Fall 1985), pp. 87-100 (96).

110. See Simon Chan, 'Sharing the Trinitarian Life', in Thomas F. Best and Günther Gassmann (eds.), *On the Way to Fuller Koinonia* (Geneva: WCC Publications, 1994), pp. 83-90.

'success' rate? There was no instance where Jesus prayed for healing that failed to take place. We, however, are tainted by sin in varying degrees and unable to discern perfectly; we sometimes simply do not know God's will in a given situation; or we are too afraid or too self-centered to enter fully into the depth of fellowship with God and others. All these may explain why the gifts operate sporadically and imperfectly. But growth in godliness is characterized by greater openness to God, death to self, and increasing ability to discern, and therefore, greater sensitivity to what God wants to do in a given situation. Pentecostals in particular need to see this pattern as the norm or ideal of Christian praxis. A normative Pentecostalism is not just intensified affections, but affections configured around the five-fold gospel, with sanctification as one of its central features. Sanctification, 'the beauty of holiness', according to Jonathan Edwards, is what gives religious affections their 'truth' character—to which the Pentecostals add power and passion.[111] But Pentecostal power and passion mean nothing if they do not issue from a life filled with the Spirit of holiness. There could be false affections and false Pentecostalisms! Spirit-baptism is inextricably bound up with a larger spiritual reality, and together they constitute the true Pentecostal way of life.

Spirit-Baptism as a Theological Perspective

When Spirit-baptism and holiness are conjoined, the Pentecostal reality is no longer just one component in the Christian life, but provides a perspective with which to view the whole of the Christian life. The Christian life can be seen in terms of the distinctive work of the Spirit in the trinitarian relationship. The Spirit indwells believers, prompting and goading them to pray to the Father as the children of God through their union with the Son (Rom. 8.15). This work of moving and inclining the believers to God corresponds to what Jonathan Edwards calls religious affections.[112] In other words, a Pentecostal spirituality is distinguished by the emphasis it gives to the affective dimension of the Christian life. Steven Land is therefore right when he argues for the centrality of the

---

111. 'True religion, in great part, consists in holy affections.' This theme was developed in the third part of Jonathan Edwards' treatise *The Religious Affections* (Edinburgh: Banner of Truth Trust, 1986 [1746]).

112. Edwards, *Religious Affections*, pp. 24-26.

'affections' in Pentecostal spirituality.[113] Spirit-baptism as the 'actualization' of the sacrament of water baptism would then mean that, from the human side, there is an awakening of the reality of God in such a manner that the religious affections are radically configured and transformed. The religious affections are quickened, deepened and intensified to provide a Pentecostal perspective of life, so that the whole spectrum of Christian living is suffused with a 'passion for the kingdom'. The Pentecostal reality is not merely one more component in the Christian life but offers a distinctive perspective for viewing the whole of that life. In other words, theology could be looked at pneumatologically, that is, from the standpoint of the Spirit's action in the believer which includes a distinctively Pentecostal dimension. Clark Pinnock in his *Flame of Love* offers one example of just such an approach to theology. His pneumatology, he tells us, is one in which the Spirit provides 'a standpoint...for surveying the whole vista of Christian truth'.[114] The Pentecostal experience is the lens through which we look at everything else rather than the direct object of our intense gaze. There is a kind of holy boldness or empowered holiness when we look at the world with a receptive attitude towards God's empowering presence.

If we compare this early Pentecostal configuration of sanctification and Spirit-baptism, we see its remarkable similarity with the ancient 'Three Ways' of spiritual progress. Conversion corresponds to the purgative way. Sanctification corresponds to the illuminative way, the phase of growth in virtues, while Spirit-baptism corresponds to the unitive way. This three-stage schema is undergirded throughout by an asceticism of 'tarrying'—a carryover of the Holiness 'penitence bench'. When Pentecostalism is interpreted within the larger Christian spiritual tradition, one begins to see its deep affinity with a normative pattern that the church has evolved over the centuries. It is this normative pattern that present-day Pentecostals need to recover and explicate more carefully if they hope to hand down the same Pentecostal fire to the next generation. Pentecostalism cannot be regarded as a marginal movement, much less an aberration; it is a spiritual movement that matches in every way the time-tested method of spiritual development in the Christian tradition. If the Pentecostal schema of spiritual progress could be successfully located within the framework of the Three Ways

113. Land, *Pentecostal Spirituality*, pp. 44-47.
114. Pinnock, *Flame of Love*, p. 10.

(as I think it could and should), then we can see that reception of the Spirit is part of a larger ascetical programme in which glossolalia functions as its most significant symbol. It is the symbol not only of passivity when it is understood as 'the initial evidence' of Spirit-baptism, but also of active pursuit of the spiritual life.

Chapter 3

PENTECOSTAL ASCETICISM

Spirit-Baptism and the Three Ways

The Pentecostal nexus of conversion, sanctification and Spirit-baptism bears strong *structural,* though not necessarily material, similarities with the traditional Three Ways. This three-stage schema offers a better basis for Pentecostals to chart their own path of spiritual progress. This path of spiritual progress is not a unilinear path; it could be pictured as a spiral development. Recent Catholic thought, following in the tradition of St Bonaventure, is coming more and more to see that the Three Ways are a repeatable pattern that one experiences in increasing depth in the course of spiritual growth.[1] Even within each phase or stage there are certain similar dynamics which recur progressively as the soul progresses towards union with God. In the purgative way prayer progresses from the active/ascetical phase to a more passive phase called the prayer of loving attention or prayer of simplicity. The graces or virtues formed are acquired graces, that is, they are formed through the active cooperation of the human will. The illuminative way begins with the prayer of infused recollection. This phase of spiritual development is characterized by greater receptivity and dependence on divine initiative and the infusion of grace by the Holy Spirit. Progress from acquired to infused virtues corresponds to progressive purification, first of the external senses (taste, touch, smell etc.) and then the internal senses (intellect, memory and will). The surrender to the Holy Spirit results in empowerment for mission. Materially, this phase comes closest to the Pentecostal experience of baptism in the Spirit which results in the

---

1. Mark O'Keefe, 'The Three Ways', *Studies in Formative Spirituality* 13.1 (February 1992), pp. 73-83 (76); Michael Downey (ed.), *The Dictionary of Catholic Spirituality* (Bangalore: Theological Publications of India, 1995), s.v. 'The Three Ways'. For a useful summary of the nature of the Three Ways see also s.v. 'purgation, purgative way', 'illumination, illuminative way', 'union, unitive way'.

'enduement of power for life and service'.[2] In both the purgative and illuminative ways the soul experiences alternation between consolation and desolation, joy and 'dark night'. These are experienced in growing intensity: the dark night of the senses in the purgative way is followed by the dark night of the soul and of the spirit at the end of the illuminative way before the soul reaches union with God.

The Three Ways help us to see that progression occurs in various aspects of the spiritual life. There is an increase in levels of intimacy in prayer, progressive formation of virtues or the sanctified life, and a deepening sense of desolation or dark night. We may not agree with the precise steps of spiritual progress as traditionally conceived (even mystical writers differ among themselves regarding the name and number of stages), but the Three Ways is still useful as a broad interpretative framework for understanding Pentecostal spiritual progress. For example, if Spirit-baptism is interpreted within the framework of the Three Ways as a spiralling and repetitive pattern, it could then be seen as an event which could occur at different levels of one's spiritual maturity. Spirit-baptism can occur in 'babes in Christ' as happened at Corinth as well as in more mature believers. We may expect the effects of Spirit-baptism to be different at the 'purgative' level and at the 'illuminative' level. A mature believer's receptivity to the Spirit will have a far more significant impact on his or her life and ministry compared with that of a young believer, just as the intimacy of mature lovers is quite different from the intimacy between people who have just fallen in love, or from the familiarity of a child towards its father or mother.

These spiritual dynamics show at once where Pentecostal spiritual theology may have fallen short compared to the Three Ways. The typical classical Pentecostal church's attempt to universalize Spirit-baptism as a second work of grace has meant that the experience has tended to occur only once at the earlier stage of one's spiritual life. Even though there is a teaching of 'one Spirit-baptism' and 'many fillings' the latter has not been generally regularized in Pentecostal churches. The focus is usually on the initial in-filling which is important from the point of

---

2.   Cf. Groeschel's characterization of the illuminative way: the use of affective prayer, the presence of Christ (p. 140), the gift of infused virtues (pp. 145-48) which empowers the person for witness and mission (pp. 149-150). (Benedict J. Groeschel, *Spiritual Passages: The Psychology of Spiritual Development* [New York: Crossroad, 1983].)

view of one's initiation into the Pentecostal ecclesial community. For many Pentecostals this initiatory function of Spirit-baptism is usually given a far more important place than the 'many fillings' afterward, as evidenced by the fact that in many Pentecostal churches, being 'Spirit-filled' with speaking in tongues at some point is usually regarded as one of the necessary criteria for leadership in the church (at least when it comes to the more important positions). The other criterion is, of course, conversion. Implied in these criteria for leadership is that conversion and Spirit-baptism are completed (and even datable) events.[3] In other words, these events are conceived of as progressing in a linear fashion rather than as repeatable events.

The negative consequence of this conception is not difficult to see. The radical in-breaking of the Spirit has not always been followed through to a more mature faith and love. It has tended to stop at a lower level where the sense of God's immediacy is more like that of people falling in love rather than that of mature lovers. Worse, some are forever stuck at this stage, preferring to prolong their honeymoon for as long as possible. They become obsessively taken up with signs and wonders and extraordinary phenomena. Or, to change the analogy, they hope to remain forever on Bunyan's 'Delectable Mountain'. Spirit-baptism becomes the means of entrance into the land of perpetual holiday, as seen in the way in which the modern Pentecostal-charismatic service has practically reduced the rich multi-faceted meaning of worship to just 'praise'. Implied in this liturgical reductionism is an over-realized eschatology. Neville Ward, who probably did not have the charismatics in view when he wrote his now famous work on prayer, *The Use of Praying* in 1967, calls this tendency 'a very attractive exaggeration... because it is such a true anticipation of the end of life, but it cannot be true of our life on earth'.[4] Here is where the mystical tradition has something vital to contribute to Pentecostalism: in the mystical way the devout soul must pass through the dark night of the soul and spirit between illumination and union. But Pentecostals have no place in their schema for the dark night. More often, they are likely to dismiss such

---

3.   Conversion and Spirit-baptism have the same logical function as conversion and entire sanctification for the Wesleyan-Holiness Christian. In fact, in older Methodist churches it was not uncommon to identify two classes of members: those who are saved and those who are 'entirely sanctified'.

4.   Neville Ward, *The Use of Praying* (London: Epworth Press, 1988 [1967]), p. 29.

an experience as due to a lack of faith or an attack from the devil.[5]

A broader, more biblical understanding of Spirit-baptism should lead Pentecostals to find a place not only for mystical union and joy but also for the dark night. Here von Balthasar's 'theology of Holy Saturday' could well provide them with a supreme pattern and theological basis for the dark night. Between the cross and resurrection our Lord underwent what in early Christian tradition was called the 'descent into hell' where he endured absolute solidarity with the dead, where there is 'no living communication'. 'Here solidarity means: being solitary like, and with, the others.'[6]

> Into this finality (of death) the dead Son descends, no longer acting in any way, but stripped by the cross of every power and initiative of his own, as one purely to be used, debased to mere matter, with a fully indifferent (corpse) obedience, incapable of any act of solidarity—only thus is he right for any 'sermon' to the dead.[7]

There are some things that only Christ as redeemer could do, which are his alone to bear, but (here von Balthasar is guided by Gregory of Nyssa and Thomas Aquinas) this should not hold Pentecostals back from following Christ 'at a distance'.[8] The dark night may be seen as one such experience of accompanying Christ in his 'descent into hell'.

Pentecostals have a foretaste of mystical union when their speaking in tongues signals an attitude of receptivity towards God. But they have not gone farther up the mystical way because they have shunned the path through the dark night. Here is where Pentecostalism must be open to the challenge of the mystical tradition. It must recognize that trials and spiritual aridity, even spiritual defeat and desolation, are a part of growth even *after* one's baptism in the Holy Spirit. This growth pattern, however, is not helped by an over-realized eschatology. If the Christian life is to be lived chiefly under the expectation of harnessing the powers

5.   The Doctrine Commission of the Church of England reported that most charismatics tended to believe that 'Christians should not normally be depressed and that their mood should primarily be characterized by joy'. *We Believe in the Holy Spirit*, p. 30.

6.   Hans Urs von Balthasar, *Mysterium Paschale* (trans. Aidan Nichols; Grand Rapids: Eerdmans, 1993), p. 165.

7.   Hans Urs von Balthasar, *The von Balthasar Reader* (ed. Medard Kehl and Werner Löser; trans. Robert J. Daly; New York: Crossroad, 1982), p. 153.

8.   von Balthasar, *Mysterium Paschale*, p. 181.

of the age to come for 'power evangelism' and 'power healing',[9] then it is difficult to see where the gift of grace for enduring the dark night would fit in. Progress in the Christian life may involve many dark nights and many re-fillings of the Spirit, each experienced in greater degree of intensity.

Except for the dark night, many of the essential elements of the Three Ways could actually be found in Pentecostal teachings and practices. What Pentecostals lack, however, is a coherent scheme bringing these elements together. Without a coherent theology, beliefs like 'many fillings' and progressive sanctification become isolated from the main body of the Pentecostal belief system. They fail to become a significant and regular part of the overall Pentecostal way of life. At best they are practised sporadically, at worst, they are totally neglected. What follows is an initial attempt at incorporating some of these disparate elements into the main body of the Pentecostal belief system using the Three Ways as the interpretative schema.

Ascetical Tongues

There is a basic ascetical structure in the Pentecostal understanding of spiritual progress. Pentecostals come from a tradition that used to have the habit of tarrying for the Spirit to do the work of entire sanctification and later, 'tarrying' for the baptism in the Spirit. This mood is well captured in one of their songs:

Waiting on the Lord, for the promise given;
Waiting on the Lord to send from heaven;
Waiting on the Lord, by our faith receiving;
Waiting in the upper room.
The power! The power! Gives victory over sin and purity within;
The power! The power! The pow'r they had at Pentecost.

They know by instinct that praying, fasting, seeking the Lord are all necessary conditions for spiritual progress. What is needed is for the ascetical structure to be more consciously developed, and this means basing it on sound theology. But where is the source for such a theology? The way forward for Pentecostals is actually to move along the same path in which they began their journey: the way of glossolalia.[10]

---

9. These are the titles of two of John Wimber's books.
10. Amos Yong has shown that the truth of glossolalia could be established

Pentecostals believe that tongues are not just signals of the in-breaking of divine revelation; it is also a 'prayer language' that can be exercised throughout one's life. I believe that this offers the best way for Pentecostals to develop their own distinctive path of spiritual progress.

To appreciate the ascetical dimension of glossolalia it needs to be connected to baptism in the Spirit as the sacramental sign. That is to say, there is a necessary connection between the physical act of glosso-lalia and the spiritual reality called Spirit-baptism. The connection works in two ways. When Pentecostals experience tongues as evidence, it is the spiritual reality that reveals itself, prompting or triggering the glossolalic response (as discussed in Chapter 2). It is an experience of passive or infused grace or, to borrow an expression from Barth, 'active passivity'. There is, of course, a prior asceticism of 'waiting on the Lord' to send the Pentecostal fire. But essentially tongues is a *response* to the revelation of God. The soul is briefly illuminated by the divine manifestation or theophany. But glossolalia is also an on-going practice in the Spirit-filled believer. The Christian who is overwhelmed by the divine presence spontaneously responds in tongues; at the same time the glossolaliac discovers an 'idiolect'[11] which helps him or her to express the inexpressible in prayer. When tongues are exercised contin-ually as the language of prayer, they become the 'occasion' for a new theophany and a new level of intimacy with God. Tongues function as a means of grace.

Some modern charismatics may have conceived of tongues as means of grace in rather crude, quasi-magical terms, as when they say that speaking in tongues ensures that the message is properly and cryptically encoded by the Holy Spirit so that the principalities and powers of the air will not be able to intercept it. Tongues are the language for spiritual warfare![12] I suspect that this kind of sacramental explanation is no better than popular mediaeval superstitions about the sacraments.

---

precisely when it is seen as a central symbol of the whole Pentecostal spiritual life which Yong structures in three stages: innocence, growth and adept. ('"Tongues of Fire" in the Pentecostal Imagination', pp. 49-62.)

11. The idea of tongues as idiolect is suggested by Ernest Best, 'The Interpreta-tion of Tongues', in Watson E. Mills (ed.), *Speaking in Tongues* (Grand Rapids: Eerdmans, 1988), pp. 295-312 (307).

12. I must confess that I do not have a published source for this. But it is cer-tainly found in popular oral tradition. I have heard it expressed more or less in those terms.

A more helpful way of seeing the relationship is in terms of C.S. Lewis' concept of transposition. Lewis observed that when a higher reality like joy is expressed through a lower medium via the physical sensation, what comes through may appear to be *no more than* physical sensations. An aesthetic experience in a concert hall may have the same physical sensation as a pain in the stomach. Yet it is a different kind of pain: it is actually *enjoyable*! Lewis' illuminating example illustrates the sacramental principle in at least two ways. First, the spiritual can be transposed into the physical, and the physical can convey the spiritual. Spiritual and physical realities are not inherently opposed to each other. This is simply incarnational theology. There is a sense in which the physical could be said to contain the spiritual. Tongues, as we have noted in the previous chapter, can be understood in terms of Rahner's 'primordial word', which is also characteristically sacramental.

> [T]he primordial word is in the proper sense the presentation of the thing itself. It is not merely the sign of something whose relationship to the hearer is in no way altered by it; it does not speak merely 'about' a relationship of the object in question to the hearer: it brings it before us. Naturally the manner of this presentation will be of the most diverse kinds, depending upon the kind of reality evoked and the power of the evoking word. But whenever a primordial word of this kind is pronounced, something happens: the advent of the thing itself to the listener.[13]

Second, even though this analogy does not explain *how* the physical and spiritual are related, it explains *why* when we say that the spiritual is conveyed through the physical in the sacramental union, the physical, sacramental sign will look very much the same as any other physical things: bread and wine in holy communion will remain very much bread and wine; tongues (most types anyway, except in the rare event of xenolalia) will always sound gibberish from the human perspective. Yet, out of ordinary bread and wine, out of ordinary gibberish, something *happens* to us: God has graced the bread and wine; God has graced the gibberish! Thus we should not be too surprised if told that studies of the linguistic patterns of glossolalia have not turned out anything significant. Theologically, it does not really matter what tongues are 'from below', that is, from the perspective of psychology, sociology or linguistics. Sometimes biblical scholars appear to be chasing a red herring when they argue over whether tongues in the New Testament

13. Rahner, *Theological Investigations*, III, p. 299.

are actual languages or simply language-like phenomena, whether tongues at Pentecost are the same as tongues in 1 Corinthians 12–14, whether the 'unutterable groanings' in Rom. 8.26 are tongues or something else. Such questions are theologically quite irrelevant. The important question is how tongues function or what they signify, that is, what spiritual reality they convey. Ultimately glossolalia cannot be interpreted in isolation from the web of meaning that it possesses in relation to other significant theological symbols within a unified biblical pattern of meaning.

If tongues are also ascetical prayer, they belong to the whole of the life of faith and not just to some initial experience of spiritual ecstasy. Prayer, as St Teresa of Avila has taught us in *The Interior Castle*, undergirds the whole of the Christian life, from start to finish. Baptism in the Holy Spirit, therefore, is initiation into a life-long and on-going life of prayer where tongues are freely spoken as part of the total life of prayer. The Pentecostal reality is not just the beginning but also the goal of the Christian life. Glossolalia symbolizes both initiation and goal, a way of life oriented around 'the surprising works of God'. It does not mean that the Christian life must consist of one surprise after another—that will either take away the surprises or it will make life quite intolerable. Being a Pentecostal does not mean that they must 'expect a miracle from God each day'—if miracle is taken in its strict theological sense. It does mean, however, that they should be open to the unpredictable. God can surprise us because he is intensely and intimately personal. As G.K. Chesterton reminded us, the very nature of being a normal person is that he or she is free to do things sometimes for no particular reason. It is the lunatic who looks for a reason in everything. When he sees someone playfully slashing the grass with his walking stick or kicking his heels, he concludes that some conspiracy must be going on: an attack on private property or a signal to an accomplice.[14] But a more sensible conclusion is that this man is simply enjoying his evening walk. There is a certain aimless 'playfulness' in the Pentecostal way of life, especially in the area of worship. I will take up this theme again later.

Glossolalia supremely embodies this particular way of life. Much of life is predictable. But pure predictability will be a drudge. If anything, the existential *angst* in modern society shows that pure predictability is

14. G.K. Chesterton, *Orthodoxy* (Garden City, NY: Image Books, 1959), pp. 18-19.

a particularly dangerous modern disease—and so is pure predictability in the modern church. Life, real life, always has a measure of unpredictability. Pentecostalism simply affirms the normalcy of such a life and glossolalia initiates and confirms us in that life. Pentecostals, of course, do not only pray in tongues; they pray with the understanding also. Their lives consist of a good mix of regular habits as well as surprises. Glossolalia, in short, represents the discovery of what is, after all, very normal Christian living.

But how does glossolalia function within the total life of prayer? The two functions of tongues—tongues as evidence and as means of grace—do not suggest that the sense of receptivity experienced in the initial Spirit-baptism is a once-for-all, unrepeatable event, any more than that the Three Ways are once-for-all events. Pentecostal ascetics thus will sometimes speak in tongues quite deliberately as a means of cultivating intimacy with God through an act of *anamesis*. This is quite essential, as McDonnell reminds us:

> The dry-mechanical ritual of tongues is an invitation to the believer to sustain himself on the memory of Jesus who was almost perceptibly present, to nurture himself in that dry but living faith which is our daily lot when Jesus manifests himself as though he were the absent one. This too is a kind of intimacy.[15]

But in the course of doing so, they may find themselves being drawn into God in such a manner that the will becomes less and less active until finally they cross the threshold and let the tongue speak, as it were, on its own accord. Pentecostal ascetics do not wait passively for God to move them before they speak; they simply pray and in the course of praying they will find themselves moving from activity to passivity. This repeatable pattern of prayer intensifies as the ascetic increases in spiritual proficiency. It is possible that this process will move him or her towards greater and greater simplification of tongues.[16] Perhaps over time a monosyllabic sound or groan would suffice to communicate the depth of the human-divine encounter, until finally silence reigns as the soul loses itself in 'wonder, love and praise'.[17]

---

15. McDonnell, 'Function of Tongues', p. 341.

16. See John Kildahl, *The Psychology of Speaking in Tongues* (New York: Harper & Row, 1972), p. 60.

17. The Doctrine Commission noted that for some charismatics 'silence could actually be the 'point' or 'end' of tongues, that to which tongues naturally lead' (*We Believe in the Holy Spirit*, p. 30).

Such a pattern of prayer is not just a Pentecostal innovation. One will find a similar devotional practice in a form of prayer which many early Orthodox writers highly recommended: the Jesus Prayer. In *The Way of a Pilgrim*, the Jesus Prayer was commended as a means to learn the secret of continual prayer. The pilgrim was advised to repeat the Jesus Prayer with increasing frequency up to 12,000 times a day. Then, one morning, it happened. Here are the pilgrim's own words:

> Once, early in the morning the Prayer seemed to awaken me. I got up to read my morning prayers, but my tongue had difficulty in formulating the words and I was overwhelmed with the desire to recite the Jesus Prayer. And when I started it, it became so easy and delightful that my tongue and lips seemed to do it of themselves.[18]

It ought to give Pentecostals no small comfort when they realize that what they had been practising spontaneously in a rather unreflective manner is remarkably akin to something which has a long history in the Christian tradition. Tongues function for the Pentecostal as silence did for the mystic and the Jesus Prayer did for the Russian pilgrim. If Pentecostals can locate the logical function of glossolalia within the larger Christian tradition it would provide a surer basis for its use and ensure that it will have a significant place in their own devotional life.

Profile of a Pentecostal Ascetic

It is generally acknowledged in the Christian spiritual tradition that prayer is the most basic ascetical practice. According to *The Way of A Pilgrim* 'prayer is both the first step and crown of a devout life'.[19] If prayer is the ultimate basis on which all ascetical practices are built[20] then Pentecostal spirituality, distinguished by glossolalic prayer, ought to be characterized by as robust an asceticism as that practised by the desert fathers. What will be the shape of a Pentecostal asceticism? I would like to answer this question by creating a profile of an ideal Pentecostal ascetic.

Pentecostal ascetics are no less rigorous than the desert monks in the school of prayer. But unlike their desert counterparts, their solitude is

---

18. Anon, *The Way of a Pilgrim*, p. 22.
19. Anon, *The Way of a Pilgrim*, p. 131.
20. See Simon Chan, *Spiritual Theology: A Systematic Study of the Christian Life* (Downers Grove, IL: InterVarsity Press, 1998), pp. 125-40.

not achieved by physically removing themselves from the human community. Through glossolalia they practise mental solitude. They withdraw into the desert within and enter into a personal intimacy with God. This is how they understand 1 Cor. 14.2, 4 to mean: 'He who speaks in a tongue does not speak to men but to God' and 'He who speaks in a tongue edifies himself.'[21]

From the desert fathers, they learn to operate the gifts of the Spirit, especially the gift of charismatic discernment in the area of spiritual direction.[22] They recognize, as the Russian staretz does, that we are dealing with the deepest area of human existence: the human spirit, 'an area of mystery and awe' as Tildern Edwards puts it,[23] and so nothing less than the complete reliance on God is needed. Their deep communion with God helps them to see their own heart and also the heart of others. Occasionally, they will speak a surprising word of wisdom that is not learned from books, but from 'inspiration'.[24] In Pentecostal parlance, this is a 'prophetic word from the Lord'. Many of the desert fathers too, have uttered such prophetic words as can be gleaned from their aphoristic 'sayings'. Their words often contain gems of wisdom which were later used in institutionalized monasticism as subjects for fruitful meditation. The monk would, in the course of the day, dwell on one of these sayings, allowing it to run through the mind over and over again.[25] These sayings are appropriately called *florelegia*:[26] flowers

21. Fee believes that the above verses refer to a non-rational kind of communion: 'Paul believed in an immediate communing with God by means of the S/spirit that sometimes bypassed the mind' (*God's Empowering Presence*, p. 219).

22. Kallistos Ware, 'The Spiritual Director in Orthodox Christianity', in Kevin G. Culligan, O.C.D. (ed.), *Spiritual Direction: Contemporary Readings* (Locus Valley, NY: Living Flame, 1983), pp. 21-23.

23. Tildern Edwards, *Spiritual Friend: Reclaiming the Gift of Spiritual Direction* (New York: Paulist Press, 1980), p. 212.

24. Benedicta Ward (trans.), *Sayings of the Desert Fathers: The Alphabetical Collections* (Kalamazoo, MI: Cistercian Publications, 1975) and *The Wisdom of the Desert Fathers: Apophthegmata Patrum* (Oxford: SLG Press, 1975).

25. For a study of this practice, see Irénée Hausherr, *The Name of Jesus: The Names of Jesus Used by Early Christians. The Development of the 'Jesus Prayer'* (trans. Charles Cummings; Kalamazoo, MI: Cistercian Publications, 1978), pp. 172-80.

26. See Jean Leclercq, *The Love of Learning and the Desire for God* (New York: Fordham University Press, 1985), pp. 182-84; Hausherr, *The Name of Jesus*, p. 177.

from which the diligent bee draws out sweetness. A parallel phenomenon can be found in the Pentecostal practice of singing a short chorus over and over. Sometimes these choruses are derived from previously uttered 'prophetic words'.

The Pentecostal ascetics also 'sing in the Spirit'. Francis Sullivan has noted that this singing in the Spirit or singing in tongues is remarkably similar to what the ancients called the *jubilus*, of which there is a succinct description in Augustine.

> What does it mean to sing in jubilation? It means to realize that you cannot express in words what your heart is singing. People who are singing, for example, during the harvest or the vintage or some other such ardent work, who have begun to exult with joy in the words of a song, as if filled with such great joy that they can no longer express it in words, leave off the syllables of words and go into the sound of jubilation. For jubilation is a sound which signifies that the heart is giving utterance to what it cannot say in words. And for whom is such jubilation fitting if not for the ineffable God? For he is ineffable whom one cannot express in words; and if you cannot express Him in words, and yet you cannot remain silent either, then what is left but to sing in jubilation, so that your heart may rejoice without words, and your unbounded joy may not be confined by the limits of syllables.[27]

The Pentecostal ascetics pray for the sick and they are healed, but give no special attention to the fact that a miracle has occurred.[28] They also learn from the desert tradition that the gifts of the Spirit are not just the *gratia data gratis*, the free flow of God's grace apart from one's own sanctification, but also an overflow of a life 'full of grace and truth'.[29]

Above all, the Pentecostal ascetics' life is characterized by the eschatological groaning for the kingdom of God (Rom. 8.26). They find their praying with 'unutterable groanings' drawing them ineluctably to iden-

---

27. Sullivan, *Charisms and Charismatic Renewal*, p. 147.

28. Cf. the attitude of Sadhu Sundar Singh towards healing as noted above, p. 66. This is not to suggest that Sundar Singh could be classified as a Pentecostal-charismatic, but that his approach to healing and miracles could well serve as a model for the Pentecostal ascetic.

29. The miraculous issuing from a holy life is amply illustrated in the life of St Anthony. After spending twenty years in solitude 'he came forth initiated in the mysteries and filled with the Spirit of God'. Henceforth, miracles began to occur through him. Noted in Stanley M. Burgess, *The Holy Spirit: Ancient Christian Tradition* (Peabody, MA: Hendriksen Press, 1984), p. 121.

tify themselves with the birth pangs of creation. They feel keenly the pain of a fallen creation and of the oppressed, and they pray in hope for freedom. If the Pentecostal ascetics come close to experiencing the 'dark night' it will probably be through their intense engagement in intercessory prayer in the Spirit. In this engagement they discover that their hope is not of this world. Worldly utopias are not the eschatological kingdom of God. For the Spirit within gives them a foretaste of the heavenly hope that will be fulfilled in the new creation.

My 'ideal type' portrait of the Pentecostal ascetic helps us to see that there is great scope for interpreting the Pentecostal reality within the larger Christian spiritual tradition without diluting the Pentecostal heritage. Rather, by so doing Pentecostals will strengthen their heritage, especially those features that are practically abandoned (like tongues) and those features that have been distorted by the uncritical assimilation of modern culture, such as the 'kingdom now' theology.

The Doctrine of Subsequence

All the distinct characteristics of the Pentecostal way of life can be strengthened if they are seen as part of a structured path of spiritual growth. To do this, we need once again to rethink the doctrine of subsequence. The traditional Pentecostal understanding of subsequence has been severely criticized by evangelicals because it is seen as a *superadditum* to being saved, thus implying that the work of grace at conversion is somewhat incomplete. But in recent years this traditional Pentecostal doctrine has been cogently defended by a number of Pentecostal scholars, most notably Robert Menzies. The defence, basically, is to argue for a distinctive Lukan pneumatology. According to Menzies, Luke's understanding of Spirit-filling is strictly missiological and has no soteriological functions at all.[30] By maintaining this strict demarcation in Lukan pneumatology, it is possible not only to show the logical relationship between glossolalia and Spirit-baptism,[31] it also makes the doctrine of subsequence a more feasible option. As Menzies has quite rightly pointed out, 'if my description of Luke's "distinctive" pneumatology is accurate, then Luke's intent to teach a Spirit-baptism distinct

---

30. Menzies, *Empowered for Witness*, pp. 235-36.

31. As noted above, p. 48. If Luke sees Spirit-filling as strictly to empower the church for mission, then glossolalia would certainly function as an appropriate symbol.

from conversion for empowering is easily demonstrated'.[32] It is then conceivable to see the Christian life as consisting of two phases: a Pauline phase consisting of the Spirit's work of conversion-initiation and the bestowal of the charisms, and a Lukan phase consisting of the special work of empowerment for mission. These two phases, even if they are not always sequential, could be seen as at least distinct from each other.

While I share the concerns of Menzies regarding the doctrine of subsequence, there are two reasons why I think a defence of the doctrine along the lines Menzies has suggested is not sustainable. First, it is premised on a position that is still highly debatable in Lukan scholarship. It depends very much upon making a clear demarcation between Luke and Paul. According to Menzies, 'Luke *never* attributes soteriological functions to the Spirit' while Paul frequently speaks of the soteriological dimension of the Spirit's work.[33] While many scholars, I think, would agree that Luke's pneumatology focuses mainly on the missiological dimension, not many would take the view that it has no soteriological functions at all.[34] Also, Menzies's conclusion is derived from a redactional reading of Luke,[35] and there may well be other ways of reading Luke from which different conclusions could be drawn.[36] Second, as a way of structuring the Christian life it is inadequate. I have pointed out earlier that a doctrine of initial evidence based on a missiological interpretation of Spirit-baptism lacks wider contextual grounding as it leaves out the dimension of personal relationship. The same can be said of a doctrine of subsequence. Inevitably empowerment comes to be identified with the growth process itself. For if empower-

---

32. Menzies, *Empowered for Witness*, p. 239.

33. Menzies, *Empowered for Witness*, p. 237. Emphasis mine.

34. For example, Turner, *The Holy Spirit*, pp. 46-56; Shelton, *Mighty in Word and Deed*, pp. 158-60; William Atkinson, 'Pentecostal Responses to Dunn's Baptism in the Holy Spirit: Luke–Acts', *Journal of Pentecostal Theology* 6 (1995), pp. 87-131. Atkinson sees Menzies's position as 'too narrow' (pp. 122-23). See a similar conclusion by Archie Hui, 'The Spirit of Prophecy and Pauline Pneumatology', *Tyndale Bulletin* 50.1 (1999), pp. 93-115.

35. It is noteworthy that both Turner and Shelton use the same redactional approach, yet come to slightly different conclusions from Menzies'.

36. Cf. the essays of Larry W. Hurtado, 'Normal, but Not a Norm: Initial Evidence and the New Testament', pp. 189-201 and J. Ramsey Michaels, 'Evidences of the Spirit, or the Spirit as Evidence? Some Non-Pentecostal Reflections', pp. 202-207 both in McGee (ed.), *Initial Evidence*.

ment is the second phase of the Spirit's work after the crisis conversion, it is only one small step from identifying the gift of power as representing a further advance in the spiritual life. Empowerment, rather, should be understood as a *result* of spiritual growth, as is the case in the Three Ways where empowerment comes in the Illuminative Way in relation to virtue formation, and in Wesleyan-Pentecostalism where it comes after entire sanctification. One could still speak of Spirit-baptism as empowerment for witness only if this dimension of the Spirit's work is understood as an outcome of life in the Spirit. This was the way that the sacrament of confirmation was understood traditionally.[37] In fact, without the intervening work of sanctification, the Reformed Pentecostal view could in the long term bring more harm than good. Power can easily become corrupting when it is divorced from holiness—more so, when it is confused with spiritual maturity.

The way forward for the Pentecostal teaching on subsequence is to locate it within the conversion-initiation complex. But conversion must be seen as a process of development rather than just a crisis experience. The problem with the evangelical concept of conversion is that it concludes from the theological oneness of conversion-initiation and Spirit-baptism that the Christian life is only a matter of getting saved and then getting more and more 'Christ-like' without any clear understanding of what Christ-likeness consists of and how it is to be realized. This problem is encapsulated in popular evangelicalism's concept of crisis conversion which has become an entrenched part of its belief system. The early Pentecostals had inherited this concept, and consequently, the doctrine of Spirit-baptism as 'distinct from and subsequent to' conversion simply followed with inevitable logic. The problem of the Pentecostal doctrine of subsequence arises precisely because they share a faulty doctrine of conversion with their fellow-evangelicals. But with the charismatic renewal, this Pentecostal experience has forced a redefinition of conversion as seen in the 1977 joint statement of charismatic and evangelical Anglicans. Here we see a more comprehensive term 'Christian initiation' being used instead of conversion. Initiation is understood as 'a unitary work with many facets' and 'is itself apprehended and experienced by different individuals in different ways and time-scales'.[38] No longer can we think of Christian initiation as purely a

37. See below, pp. 91-93.
38. Cited by Henry Lederle, *Treasures Old and New* (Peabody, MA: Hendrickson Press, 1988), p. 145.

once-for-all event. It must include some kind of progression as part of its essential meaning. If this is the case, then evangelicals and Pentecostals cannot stop at a hazy reconceptualization of conversion as progression; they must follow the lead of the larger Christian tradition in understanding this progression in terms of some discernible stages of spiritual development.

By 'stages of spiritual development' I do not mean that we can draw the line where one crosses from one stage to another. These are conceptual stages within the larger unified life in Christ, and may be compared to, for example, Teresa of Avila's seven 'mansions' of the 'interior castle' of prayer or her four degrees of prayer in her autobiography. Evangelicals tend to see the Christian life as one big, indistinct blob. One is expected to grow, but what is the expected pattern of development remains at best a hazy notion. A common pattern, if it could be called a pattern, goes something like this: first, conversion, followed by three months of follow-up and discipling where one is taught the basic techniques of 'quiet time' and witnessing. Then one is expected to serve the Lord faithfully to the end of one's life. It is no wonder that evangelicals have not produced a spiritual theology that understands Christian progress in terms of some structure of growth. What many evangelicals have done is to baptize one of the current theories in 'developmental psychology' and use it for structuring their own spiritual life.[39] The result has often been quite disastrous. Christian life is turned into a weak version of pop psychology. Thus there are those who think that a two-stage theory of the Christian life is unbiblical, but are quite ready to embrace the idea that spiritual maturity means having a healthy self-image, or a life patterned according to the vision of Abraham Maslow, Erick Erikson or Lawrence Kohlberg!

The importance of the doctrine of subsequence is that properly understood it provides the basis for sound spiritual development. It preserves vital aspects of the Christian life by giving these aspects a distinct focus. This is what the Wesleyan multi-stage theory of the Christian life accomplishes, which the Pentecostals inherited. But its roots

39. E.g. Erik Erikson, *Identity and the Life Cycle: Selected Papers* (New York: International Universities Press, 1959); *idem, The Life Cycle Completed* (New York: Norton, 1982); Lawrence Kohlberg, *The Psychology of Moral Development: The Nature and Validity of Moral Stages* (San Francisco: Harper & Row, 1984); James Fowler, *Stages of Faith: The Psychology of Human Development and the Quest for Meaning* (San Francisco: Harper & Row, 1981).

are much deeper in the mystical tradition of the church where it is variously named and developed: the beginner-proficient-perfect schema of Evagrius Ponticus (346–399); the four degrees of love of St Bernard, the seven mansions of Teresa of Avila. But mostly it is called the Three Ways, following Pseudo-Dionysius (c. 500): purgation, illumination and union.

Without some such doctrine of subsequence or distinctness, evangelicals wishing to preserve some of the desirable elements of the Pentecostal-charismatic movement, despite their best intentions, will not succeed in doing so in the long term. Turner, for example, thinks that one can maintain the essential features of the Pentecostal reality without a 'second blessing' theology.[40] Turner would like to see some kind of deepening, some 'degree' of development in conversion-initiation without specifying any 'kind' of change.[41] There may even be a difference between the Spirit's working for the benefit of the believers and the Spirit's working through the believers, but this is regarded as 'an irrelevant distinction'.[42] Turner is right only in the sense that conversion-initiation must be seen as a unified reality. But from the standpoint of spirituality Turner's position is highly problematic. First, the distinction Turner makes is traditionally identified as the *gratia gratum faciens* (sanctifying grace) and the *gratia gratis data* (grace given for service), and it is by no means irrelevant. It is the basis by which Christian tradition distinguishes the two kinds of miracles as noted in the previous chapter in Thomas Aquinas. Second, when Spirit-baptism is collapsed into conversion-initiation without specifying the distinct realities that it contains, spiritual development remains one big, indistinct blob. The danger that this poses is that in time the distinctive experience of Spirit-baptism will be lost. We see this happening earlier (see pp. 68-69) when the Reformed Pentecostals collapsed sanctification into the conversion complex. In time, sanctification loses its distinctive character and focus. A position that grounds Spirit-baptism experientially in conversion will eventually lose its distinctive qualities unless conversion itself is interpreted in such a way as to highlight those realities contained in the concept of Spirit-baptism.

This has been done, for the most part, in the sacramental traditions where Christian initiation is seen in two distinct acts: baptism and

---

40. Turner, *The Holy Spirit*, p. 167.
41. Turner, *The Holy Spirit*, pp. 350, 356-58.
42. Turner, *The Holy Spirit*, p. 156.

confirmation. The relationship between the two rites have been variously described. One could speak of confirmation as the 'actualization' of the Spirit given at baptism.[43] Or one could see the two rites as bearing different relations to the different persons of the Trinity. According to Ives Congar, confirmation signifies that the Holy Spirit is distinct from the Word: we are baptized into Christ, confirmed by the Spirit. It also 'points to the fact that Jesus received two anointings of the Spirit, the first constituting his human and divine holy being and the second constituting, or at least declaring, his quality of Messiah or minister of salvation'. The apostles too were first constituted by their call which took place at their baptism; then they were sent (*apostello*) as witnesses and founders of the church at Pentecost.[44] Coincidentally, Congar's view of confirmation comes close to Menzies's view of Spirit-baptism in Luke–Acts. But for Congar confirmation is part of Christian initiation. Actualization of the charisms is something that must grow out of the life of faith, rather than something added to it. Or, one could understand confirmation as symbolizing the awakening of another level of the divine presence. Although Francis Sullivan does not link Spirit-baptism with confirmation, yet, building on the teaching of Aquinas that God can be present in different ways, he nonetheless sees Spirit-baptism as indicating another dimension of God's presence in the believer.[45] All these descriptions suggest a certain distinctness about the Pentecostal experience, even a kind of quantum leap in the divine-human encounter. Something else is now being realized which was not realized before.

Confirmation clarifies the Pentecostal concept of the 'second (or third) work of grace' while interpreting this subsequent 'constitution' by the Spirit within the unified theological reality of Christian initiation. Confirmation should not be seen as a sacrament that completes the sacrament of water baptism. This would suggest that confirmation is a kind of *superadditum* to a somewhat deficient conversion, and would suffer from the same criticism levelled at the classical Pentecostal doctrine of a two-stage development. Rather, the Spirit should be seen as objectively given at baptism, but its actualization occurs subsequently in confirmation. Now, if confirmation is an actualization, then it should

---

43. E.g. Robert M. Price, 'Confirmation and Charisma', *St Luke's Journal of Theology* 23.3 (June 1990), pp. 173-83 (181-82).

44. Congar, *I Believe in the Holy Spirit*, I, p. 106.

45. Sullivan, *Charisms and Charismatic Renewal*, pp. 69-70.

be observed as more than a mere ritual but an occasion where the candidate is prayed for specifically to receive the empowering presence of the Spirit.[46]

Remarkably, this experiential aspect of Christian initiation was developed quite early in the church, for example, in Tertullian in his treatise *On Baptism* prior to his becoming a Montanist.[47] Tertullian saw the whole process of Christian initiation as involving a number of discrete rites. At baptism, the candidate underwent the 'water-bath', followed by the imposition of hands (confirmation), and then the candidate partook his or her first communion. It was after the 'water-bath' that the candidate was encouraged to pray to receive the *charisms*.[48] This was no mere ritual, but along with the prayer with outstretched arms, the newly baptized was expected to experience some observable manifestation of the charisms.[49]

> Therefore, you blessed ones, for whom the grace of God is waiting, when you come up from the most sacred bath of the new birth, when you spread out your hands for the first time in your mother's house with your brethren, ask your Father, ask your Lord, for the special gift of his inheritance, the distributed charisms, which form an additional, underlying feature [of baptism]. Ask, he says, and you shall receive. In fact, you have sought, and you have found: you have knocked, and it has been opened to you.[50]

The doctrine of confirmation helps us to appreciate the experiential difference between conversion and Spirit-baptism. The difference may be compared to that of a seed and a tree. An acorn is a potential oak; an oak developed from an acorn. But it would be quite inappropriate to call a hundred year old oak a very, very large acorn, or simply a further 'extension' of an acorn. The language of distinctness and subsequence is truer to the nature of Spirit-baptism in Scripture and in the Christian tradition than the description that sees it simply as an enlargement or

46. Price, 'Confirmation and Charisma', pp. 181-82. Price's interpretation of Lukan pneumatology is very similar to Stronstad and Menzies's, except that he ties the subsequent or distinct Spirit-baptism (as in Acts 10) to confirmation, and therefore is able to interpret it as part of Christian initiation (pp. 174-81).

47. *On Baptism* has been variously dated from as early as 198 to as late as 212. See McDonnell and Montague, *Christian Initiation*, p. 111-12.

48. McDonnell and Montague, *Christian Initiation*, pp. 98-105.

49. McDonnell and Montague, *Christian Initiation*, p. 104.

50. McDonnell and Montague, *Christian Initiation*, p. 98.

appropriation of conversion-initiation. It is certainly consistent with the richness and diversity of trinitarian faith. In confirmation one is made aware of a different level of personal presence and even a different relationship to a different person of the Trinity, as noted above. We might even stretch this biological analogy to include a third phase: not only does an acorn grow to become an oak, the tree continues its growth to bear fruit. For many the subsequent experience may include, besides the actualization of conversion, the actualization of the charisms and empowerment for service. The biological analogy could be further complemented by the social analogy. Spirit-baptism is like entering the world of play, and growth in the Christian life is developing a growing capacity to move freely to and from the world of ordinary living and the world of play.

Low church evangelicals, lacking such a sacramental tradition, are left without any adequate conceptual tools to clarify the nature of spiritual progress. Turner's position, and most other evangelicals', I fear, will not have the capacity for long-term traditioning of the Pentecostal dimension of life. As the history of Protestantism shows, the vitality of conversion could easily be reduced to a benign concept. Many Puritans in the seventeenth century developed a concept called 'the seal of the Spirit' as a distinct experience of assurance of salvation, but over time its distinctiveness was lost as it was absorbed into the popular evangelical concept of crisis conversion.[51]

Some kind of doctrine specifying the experiential distinctiveness of Spirit-baptism is needed for the long-term survival of the Pentecostal-charismatic reality. Pentecostals could learn something from the sacramentalists who have incorporated the Pentecostal distinctiveness into their sacraments of baptism and confirmation. Evangelicals are quite understandably suspicious of a theology that ties the grace of God too closely to the sacraments.[52] But properly understood, a sacramental

---

51. See Lederle, *Treasures Old and New*, pp. 5-9. A twentieth-century attempt at reviving this concept can be seen in Martin Lloyd-Jones, *Joy Unspeakable: Baptism with the Holy Spirit* (Eastbourne, E. Sussex: Kingsway Publications, 1984).

52. Turner, for example, is rather dismissive towards the sacramental interpretation, and quotes with approval Lederle's view that sees Spirit-baptism as the 'actualization' of grace already given in the sacrament of baptism does not quite do justice to the powerful experiential reality of Spirit-baptism (*The Holy Spirit*, p. 163). It is of interest to note that the Catholic Francis Sullivan voiced the same reservation (*Charisms and Charismatic Renewal*, pp. 69-70).

view of Spirit-baptism has the advantage of preserving the distinctiveness of the Pentecostal experience (which the two-stage theory tries also to do) and at the same time grounding the experience in the doctrine of conversion-initiation.

Pentecostals, having no sacrament of confirmation, nevertheless seek to preserve the experience of Spirit-baptism in their doctrine of subsequence. Perhaps the doctrine of subsequence is too simplistic a way of encapsulating the complex realities within the Christian growth process. But what we need is a better doctrine and not its abandonment if the consequence is the reduction of the richness and diversity of the Christian life to an indistinct blob commonly seen in the evangelical concept of crisis conversion. One practical step that Pentecostals might want to consider in order to appreciate better the doctrine of subsequence as part of the complex of conversion-initiation is to have the prayer for the Spirit's filling to be carried out during the water baptismal ritual. Pentecostals are sometimes impatient for converts to be filled with the Spirit as soon as possible. But there is no reason why the prayer could not be delayed until some teaching is given to the new converts as part of their preparation for baptism. It would certainly help to correct the mistaken notion that Spirit-baptism is some kind of *superadditum* and confirm the truth that it grows out of the conversion-initiation complex.

Another advantage of the sacramental interpretation is that it provides an adequate symbol for initiating one into the practice of continuous in-filling. The concept of 'many fillings' is generally acknowledged to be a biblical one. Fee sees it in Paul's linking together the reception of the Spirit with the continuous 'supply of the Spirit' and the working of miracles in Gal. 3.5. In so doing, Paul implies that 'even though they have received the Spirit [at conversion], there is another sense in which God "supplies" the Spirit again and again'.[53] Similarly, Turner believes that believers who receive the Spirit at conversion may yet have many 'refreshings' of the Spirit.[54] The Pentecostal-charismatic reality is seen as a fresh and dynamic coming of the Spirit. One must ask the non-sacramentalists, however, how their interpretation has any advantage over the sacramentalists' teaching of many 'actualizations' of grace already given at baptism.[55] The non-sacramental view still leaves unexplained how there could be many 'refreshings' when the Spirit is

53. Fee, *God's Empowering Presence*, p. 388.
54. Turner, *The Holy Spirit*, pp. 153-54.
55. Cf. n. 52 above.

already received at conversion. Unlike the sacramental interpretation, the non-sacramental view does not specify any discrete acts within conversion-initiation, and therefore the 'many fillings' do not raise any expectation of a distinct experiential reality. The fresh coming of the Spirit could just as well be seen as no more than a further extension of the Spirit's work begun at conversion. If the Spirit is already dwelling in the believer at conversion, then whether he or she has the 'supernatural' *charismata* or the more 'natural' ones is very much the result of the sovereign work of the Spirit. Maybe for some, the Spirit chooses to work quietly rather than visibly. One could still speak of 'many fillings' without pointing to any particular experiential reality. We are back to a situation where Spirit-filling is reduced to a benign concept. I am not saying that this is the way evangelicals usually interpret Spirit-baptism, but it is what their interpretation tends to end up as.

A sacramental interpretation of 'many fillings' connects the events to a certain sacramental ritual. The way open to classical Pentecostals is to locate the *repeatable* events of the Spirit's in-filling in the sacrament of holy communion. Just as prayer for the experiential reality of Spirit-baptism could appropriately be made at confirmation (or, for churches that do not practise confirmation, immediately after the believer's baptism), so holy communion is the most appropriate occasion for a fresh in-filling of the Spirit. There is, in fact, a provision for this in a part of the communion ritual called the *epiclesis* when the Holy Spirit is invoked in connection with the consecration of the bread and wine: 'grant that by the power of your Holy Spirit these gifts of bread and wine may be to us his body and his blood'.[56] One could, of course, argue over what exactly the Holy Spirit does in relation to the bread and wine. Whether he 'transubstantiates' or 'consubstantiates' or illumines the believers to perceive the spiritual presence of Christ as Calvin believed—these are debatable issues. What this part of the ritual highlights is the truth that the on-going life of faith is dependent upon and sustained by the regular in-filling of the Holy Spirit. Just as the *epiclesis* is a specific prayer for a specific event, prayer for Spirit-infusion is also for a specific event to happen. There is nothing new in the idea that the holy communion could be the occasion for the powerful manifestation of God. It appears to be quite a common feature in the early Methodist experience and may explain their practice of frequent communion, a

---

56. *The Alternative Service Book* (Cambridge: Cambridge University Press, 1980), p. 131.

practice that was unprecedented at that time.[57] In one of the Wesleys' 'Hymns on the Lord's Supper' we have more than a hint of what the *epiclesis* was supposed to accomplish:

> Come, Holy Ghost, thine influence shed,
> And realise the sign;
> Thy life infuse into the bread,
> Thy power into the wine.[58]

Clearly, communion was no mere ritual for the Wesleys, but an occasion of heightened expectation of a deep spiritual encounter, as another of the Wesleys' communion hymns shows.

> Ye faithful souls, who thus record
> The passion of that Lamb divine,
> Is the memorial of your Lord
> A useless form, an empty sign?
> Or doth he here his life impart?
> What saith the witness in your heart?
>
> Is it the dying Master's will
> That we should this persist to do?
> Then let him here himself reveal,
> The token of his presence show,
> Descend in blessings from above,
> And answer by the fire of love.
>
> Who thee remember in thy ways,
> Come, Lord, and meet and bless us here;
> In confidence we ask the grace;
> Faithful and True, appear, appear,
> Let all perceive thy blood applied,
> Let all discern the Crucified.
>
> 'Tis done; the Lord sets to his seal,
> The prayer is heard, the grace is given

57. Even though the early Reformers advocated frequent communion, it was never implemented. In fact, until the Wesleys, the standard practice in most Protestant bodies was at most four times a year. The Wesleys communicated once a week, thus earning for themselves the name 'sacramentarians'. See John Wesley, *The Journal of the Rev. John Wesley, A.M.*, I (ed. Nehemiah Curnock; 8 vols.; London: Charles H. Kelly, 1909), p. 98n.

58. *John and Charles Wesley: Selected Writings and Hymns*, in Franking Whaling (ed.), *Classics of Western Spirituality* (New York: Paulist Press, 1981), p. 260.

With joy unspeakable we feel
The Holy Ghost sent down from heaven;
The altar streams with sacred blood,
And all the temple with God![59]

John Wesley in his journal recorded some rather extraordinary happenings during communion: 'Many were cut to the heart, and at the Lord's Supper many were wounded and many healed.'[60] A certain Richard Jeffs was contemplating to join the Quakers but decided to come 'once more to the Lord's Table'. No sooner had he 'received than he dropped down, and cried with a loud voice, "I have sinned; I have sinned against God". At that instant many were pierced to the heart'.[61]

Pentecostals could learn from their Methodist forebears to appropriate the experiential reality from eucharistic observances. But perhaps more important than just having a repeatable personal 'refreshing', holy communion is also the occasion for the believers corporately to be given a fresh infusion of the Spirit, making them grow more and more into the one charismatic Body of Christ. This body is a community of reconciliation and healing, and so, in the midst of the celebration the Pentecostals also anoint the sick with oil and pray for divine healing according to James 5. The church is the context in which the charisms are exercised. A church that depends on the healing prowess of some travelling evangelist has failed to take seriously the spiritual resources that are available to them by virtue of their being incorporated into the Body of Christ. What this shows is the importance of a Pentecostal ecclesiology for the Pentecostal way of life. The Pentecostal reality cannot be effectively traditioned without grounding it in ecclesiology.

59. *John and Charles Wesley*, pp. 261-62.
60. Wesley, *Journal*, 20 July 1777.
61. Wesley, *Journal*, 4 November 1744.

Chapter 4

PENTECOSTAL ECCLESIOLOGY

The Prior Existence of the Church

More than thirty years ago, the ecumenical theologian D.T. Niles had highlighted the centrality of the church.

> We often say that the answer to the problems of our world is Jesus Christ. Can I say with reverence that the answer to the problems of our world is not Jesus Christ? The answer to the problems of the world is the answer that Jesus Christ provided, which is the Church Jesus Christ has set in the world, a community bound to him, sharing his life and his mission, and endued with the power of the Holy Spirit. This community...is the answer that Jesus has provided for the evils of this world.[1]

This truth is once again being seriously reconsidered. Carl Braaten recently calls on Protestants to return to the ancient concept of mother church.[2] Cyprian's statement that he alone can have God as his Father who first has the church as his mother[3] has never really gone down well with Protestants. They tend to think of themselves as making the church ('the church is made up of believers') rather than the church making them, giving birth to them. Consequently, Protestants have tended to see the church in purely sociological terms, that is, as a reality that is dependent largely on our own actions. The church, however, is a spiritual reality that exists prior to the individual Christians—before the foundation of the world (cf. Eph. 1.4-14). They do not make the church. It is the church that makes them, giving them their special identity. For

---

1. D.T. Niles, *The Message and its Messengers* (Nashville, TN: Abingdon Press, 1966), p. 50.
2. Carl E. Braaten, *Mother Church: Ecclesiology and Ecumenism* (Minneapolis: Fortress Press, 1998).
3. Similar expressions are also found in Origen and Augustine. See Henri de Lubac, *The Motherhood of the Church* (trans. Sr. Sergia Englund, O.C.D.; San Francisco: Ignatius Press, 1971), pp. 49-50.

to be a Christian is to be identified as one who is baptized or grafted into a pre-existing reality, the Body of Christ.

The expression Body of Christ is not a metaphor for some social dynamics but a description of a spiritual reality created by the action of the triune God. To call the church the Body of Christ means that in God's economy of redemption, he called people from the old creation and reconstituted them a new creation in Christ. This body is invigorated by the Spirit of life who raised Jesus from the dead. We don't make the church. It is God's doing and we are baptized into it and nurtured by it.

Pentecostals like their Protestant counterparts share a very weak, sociological concept of the church. This has two negative consequences. First, the church tends to be seen as essentially a service provider catering to the needs of individual Christians. Rarely are individuals thought of as existing for the church. When the church is seen as existing for the individual, then the focus of ministry is on individuals: how individual needs can be met by the church. But when we see the individuals as existing for the church, the focus shifts from the individual needs to our common life in Christ: how we as the one people of God fulfil God's ultimate purpose for the universe. The church exists for the glory and praise of God. There is no higher purpose than this (Eph. 1.6, 12, 14 etc.). The consequence of giving priority to individuals over the ecclesial life has meant that, for many classical Pentecostals, the Pentecost event has come to mean primarily a personal experience of the vivifying power of God's Spirit. By contrast, the renewal movement within the Roman Catholic church has from its very inception been linked inextricably to ecclesiology. This was because the Catholic renewal was preceded by a number of theological developments linking pneumatology and ecclesiology. Prominent theologians like Yves Congar and Karl Rahner were already drawing attention to the church as the *charismatic* body of Christ long before the charismatic renewal began in 1967.[4] Second, a sociological understanding of the church tends to see the church as a community brought about by people united for a common purpose, so that the koinonia is not primarily the creation by the Spirit of God but by a kindred human spirit. The purpose could be something quite spiritual

4.   Edward O'Connor, 'The Hidden Roots of the Charismatic Renewal in the Catholic Church', in Vinson Synan (ed.), *Aspects of Pentecostal-Charismatic Origins* (Plainfields, NJ: Logos International, 1975), pp. 169-91.

like preaching the gospel, but it is still essentially the result of human action. In the final analysis, it is the people who make the church, rather than Christ who said, 'I will build my church' (Mt. 16.18).

It is imperative, therefore, for Protestants and Pentecostals in particular to start thinking about mother church. But what will this mean? Basically, it means thinking in terms of an *ecclesial* pneumatology rather than an individual pneumatology. That is to say, the primary locus of the work of the Spirit is not in the individual Christian but in the church. The coming of the Spirit on Jesus at his baptism is often regarded as a model for the Spirit's baptism of individual Christians. Rather, Jesus' baptism should be regarded as representative of the Spirit's coming upon the church, his Body. To be baptized into Christ is to be incorporated into a Spirit-filled, Spirit-empowered entity. Spirit-baptism is first an event of the church prior to its being actualized in a personalized Spirit-baptism. This is, as we have already seen, the Matthean understanding of Spirit-baptism.[5] Understanding Spirit-baptism in this way will make one more ecclesially-conscious and responsible when Spirit-baptism is 'actualized' personally. It means that the primary focus of Spirit-baptism is to actualize our communal life, our fellowship in Christ. A basic mistake in Pentecostalism is that this fact has not been more emphasized. The Pentecostal reality has tended to be understood as individualized experiences. My relationship with God is primary, while my relationship with others is secondary. But the truth of the matter is that we cannot conceive of fellowship with God apart from fellowship in God through the Spirit. There is no question of priority. Our relationship with the triune God at once brings us into the fellowship with the saints, since no real communion with God is possible without our being baptized into the Body of Christ, the church. Yet, all too often, Pentecostals are more concerned with their 'personal Pentecost' than with the corporate Pentecostal reality of which each person has a share.

A related question is whether this corporate understanding of the Christian life is better served by a hierarchical or a 'free church' type of ecclesiology. Historically, it is the hierarchical type that has given the church a stronger sense of corporate identity—an identity held together by the role of the bishop or priest as representative of Christ (*in persona Christi*) and as representative of the church (*in persona ecclesiae*). Free

---

5. McDonnell and Montague, *Christian Initiation*, pp. 15-22.

church ecclesiology, on the other hand, has tended towards the sort of problem I have just described. Historically, it has not only been plagued by frequent fragmentation, it has also not shown a very strong capacity for traditioning. One might think that the Protestant dialectic of Word and Spirit would help to establish some form of continuity. As a matter of fact, as we shall see later, the play of Spirit and Word is crucial for structuring Pentecostal spirituality. But this play cannot be carried out effectively if it is not satisfactorily located in ecclesiology. For play to continue, there must be a playground where the rules of the game are clearly established, that is, a stable traditioning structure. In the Free Church ecclesiology, Spirit and Word tend to be rather loosely related to the church because the latter is conceived of as a voluntary association. If effective traditioning is to take place, there must be a closer conjunction between Spirit, Word and Church. This conjunction has been achieved in traditional Catholicism and Eastern Orthodoxy mainly through their giving to the church a certain conditioning role. If the church is the temple of the Holy Spirit, is there not a sense in which the temple gives shape to the Spirit? If the Incarnate Word is 'incarnated' in the church by the Spirit, is there then not, in a sense, a 'self-limitation' of Christ? The Free Church tradition has justly drawn attention to abuses whenever the church attempts to domesticate the Spirit and Word. Yet, for its part, it has never quite succeeded in taming its centrifugal voluntarism, due largely to its failure to ground Word and Spirit in ecclesiology.

But recently, Miroslav Volf, in his study of ecclesiology attempts to overcome the individualistic and voluntaristic tendencies inherent in the Free Church tradition without sacrificing the Free Church principle. Volf wants to retain the corporate and organic nature of the church,[6] but at the same time he rejects the hierarchical structure of the church found in Catholicism and Orthodoxy which is based on a hierarchical structure of the Trinity. For Catholicism the unity of the church is founded on the priority given to the oneness of God: one God—one bishop—one church, whereas for Orthodoxy unity is based on the priority of the Father, the unbegotten, without origin. Volf's own ecclesiology is based on the social doctrine of the Trinity which stresses the equality of the persons in their relations, so that the unity (rather than numerical oneness) of God arises from the trinitarian *relations*.

6.   Volf, *After our Likeness*, esp. pp. 159-89.

The constitutive role of the Father (the one who begats the Son and from whom the Spirit proceeds) plays no part in the structuring of his ecclesiology.[7] Volf overcomes the individualism and voluntarism by replacing the bishop with the laity in exactly the same role.[8] First, the church is not the subject, an idea associated with the doctrine of the 'total Christ' consisting of both head and members (*Christus totus, caput et membra*); rather, the subjects are the members themselves in interdependent communion: 'Christians *are* the mother church'.[9] Second, salvation is mediated not through the bishop but through the members of the church. Third, the church is constituted by the Holy Spirit, not through the institution of officers but through 'the communal confession in which Christians speak the word of God to one another'.[10] My aim, however, is not to evaluate the relative merits of these ecclesiologies,[11] but simply to indicate their convergence on the ecclesiality of the Spirit-filled life.

7. Volf, *After our Likeness*, pp. 202-206, 216-17.
8. Volf, *After our Likeness*, p. 224.
9. Volf, *After our Likeness*, p. 166. Emphasis author's.
10. Volf, *After our Likeness*, p. 224.
11. Even though Volf's approach has succeeded to some extent in reconceptualizing the church as an *organic* unity, it is not without its problems as far as traditioning is concerned. The first is his rejection of the hierarchical understanding of the Trinity in favour of the social, egalitarian structure of the Trinity. Can an ecclesiology be adequate if the constitutive role of the Father plays no part in structuring the church? Volf thinks that the idea of the bishop *in persona Christi* and *in persona ecclesiae* would lead to the reduction of the laity's role to insignificance. But Volf could not conceive of the role of the laity in any other way because, like Moltmann, hierarchy is always associated with domination (pp. 218-18). This aversion to hierarchy is less a reflection of biblical order (how do we understand husband as 'head' of the wife as Christ is the head of the church?), but seems to betray a carryover of modern liberal democratic values. If Volf fears the abuse of power of the church officers (p. 214), the replacement of the bishop by the laity raises the spectre of the tyranny of the mob. Second, in keeping with the Free Church principle, Volf rejects the constitutive role of officers and essentially transfers that role to the whole body of believers as a charismatic community (pp. 228-33). As such he could speak of office holders as acting *in persona Christi*, but only as a charisma which is not given permanently to any persons (p. 213). Can such a fluid conception of ministry sufficiently preserve the order of the church? Third, Volf's rejection of the *Christus totus* concept can only result in a loosening of the relationship between Christ and the church, and hence in a loose conjunction of Christ, Scripture and Tradition. Can such an ecclesiology be sustainable in the long term?

A Dynamic Catholic Community

There are a number of important characteristics connected to an ecclesial pneumatology. First, when we recognize that the Spirit 'constitutes' the church, it is not a once-for-all action so that all that is needed now is to maintain its 'constitutional' status quo. On the contrary, the action of the Spirit in the church is on-going and dynamic. This is seen in the way the church understands the action of the Spirit in relation to the eucharistic celebration. The presence of the Spirit is regularly invoked in the eucharist. As Zizioulas has pointed out, it is when believers 'come together' for the Lord's supper (1 Cor. 11.18) that they are constituted anew by the Spirit as the Church of Jesus Christ.[12] In the New Testament the local congregation could therefore be described as 'the whole church' (Rom. 16.23)—which is what the word 'catholic' means—precisely because it is constituted 'whole' by the Spirit when the whole church gathers together in the name of Jesus Christ to celebrate the Communion.

The idea of the catholicity of the local congregation needs further elaboration. Zizioulas notes that in Jewish and Roman societies there were also fraternal associations similar to the Christian church. But what makes the church unique is that as an eucharistic community sharing the *one* bread and *one* cup it transcends all social and racial boundaries. 'The eucharistic community was in its composition a catholic community in the sense that it transcended not only social but also natural divisions.'[13] There is neither Jew nor Greek, slave nor free. Within a locality (say in Rome), the *whole* church gathered to break bread. It is this transcending wholeness which makes the local congregation 'catholic'. Catholicity is a concept that is first applied to the local congregation before it becomes a universal concept. The implication of this is far-reaching. For too long we have excused the lack of church unity by focusing on a universal concept of catholicity (which, of course, remains difficult to realize). But if catholicity has to do *primarily* with the wholeness of the local congregation that gathers together to share the one loaf regardless of race, culture or sex, then the problem of the lack of catholicity is far more real and urgent. To the extent that the local congregation fails to transcend its ethnocentrism, it fails to 'discern the Lord's Body' and, therefore, has fallen short of an *essential* quality: the church's catholicity—a catholicity that we claim to believe

12. Zizioulas, *Being as Communion*, p. 148.
13. Zizioulas, *Being as Communion*, p. 148.

in when we recite the Nicene Creed: 'We believe in one holy, catholic and apostolic church...'

It is in the light of the Spirit's constituting the church as catholic that we can begin to appreciate the ecumenical impulse of the Pentecostal pioneer William Seymour at the Azusa Street Mission. Seymour was a remarkable man, probably the only person at that time who clearly understood the real significance of the Pentecostal outpouring, because he saw it as the event to bring into existence a church which is marked supremely by an all-transcending catholicity. His significance in the whole history of the Pentecostal movement could not be underestimated. Douglas Nelson describes his contribution as follows:

> Amid the most racist era of a totally segregated society, a miracle happened. For the first time in history a miniature global community came together beyond the color line, meeting night and day continuously for three years, inviting everyone to enter the new life in fellowship together. The original vision for a new society—forged again in the USA during 250 years of black slave experience—became an historical reality in the church.[14]

Seymour's understanding of the Pentecostal event also helped him to see glossolalia in a far more profound way than his white counterparts. Glossolalia was not a badge to identify oneself as a Pentecostal, nor was it just a sign of a supernatural experience; it was, for Seymour, a symbol of God's bringing together into one body people from every conceivable background. As I have noted in Chapter 2, the speaking in diverse kinds of tongues is the most appropriate symbol of an event whose primary purpose was to create a church distinguished chiefly by its all-embracing inclusiveness. For a while, the Azusa Street Mission was an embodiment of that reality.

Unfortunately, this sort of ecumenical effort was not appreciated by a majority of Pentecostals, then and now. Nelson notes that the white Pentecostals in Seymour's day, blinded by their colour prejudice, had failed to grasp the importance of what Seymour represented.[15] Before long the old divisions were raised again; the true spirit of Pentecost was compromised; the catholicity of the church was undermined. In later years, the work of another Pentecostal ecumenist, David du Plessis, was to be equally misunderstood and maligned by fellow-Pentecostals. Yet these noble attempts at realizing the true spirit of Pentecost remain a

---

14. Nelson, 'For Such a Time as This', p. 11; cf. p. 204.
15. Nelson, 'For Such a Time as This', pp. 210-11.

source of great inspiration to many present-day Pentecostals who are working tirelessly towards genuine unity, such as Cecil Robeck, Jr. The cause of the failure to see the significance of the Spirit's work in effecting catholicity in the church is not only sociological but also theological. White Pentecostals, perhaps unconsciously, had tended to downplay or underestimate the black contribution during the formative stages of the Pentecostal movement. Nelson has shown that even an otherwise 'spiritually sensitive white man' like Frank Bartleman had been biased and inaccurate in his reporting of the Azusa Street happening.[16] The result of such a prejudice is that white Pentecostals began to overlook the ecclesiological dimension of Pentecost and stress the personal-experiential and missiological dimension instead: tongues became the evidence of a personal Pentecost, a personal empowerment to preach the gospel. The problem is later compounded by their uncritical alignment with the fundamentalists. Sometimes they simply added Pentecostal fervor to fundamentalistic tendencies and concerns, such as a privatized concept of salvation, an anti-liberal rhetoric and a total rejection of Roman Catholics—attitudes that still persist to this day—despite the fact that Catholic charismatics have in recent years been far more helpful than their evangelical brethren in providing solid theological arguments for their distinctive beliefs and practices (e.g. Simon Tugwell, Francis Sullivan, Peter Hocken, Kilian McDonnell *et al.*).

A Healing Community
Second, the Spirit that creates the eucharistic community transcending all social, cultural and historical boundaries also implies that this community is characterized chiefly by its work of reconciliation and healing. Paul warned the Corinthians that failure to observe the unity of the Spirit in the eucharist is failure to 'discern the Lord's body' resulting in sickness and death (1 Cor. 11.29, 30).[17] Conversely, to 'discern the Lord's body' means effecting wholeness and healing. On this basis we can understand the *traditional* practice of divine healing in the church. Gifts of healing are the fruits of catholicity. In our search for wholeness we also discover that it includes wholeness for the person as well, body,

---

16. Nelson, 'For Such a Time as This', pp. 89-95.

17. Fee thinks that there is not a direct, 'one for one' correlation between abuse of the Supper and sickness and death, that is, those who abuse were the ones who became ill, but that the presence of illness and death had something to do with the abuse of the Supper (*Corinthians*, p. 565).

mind and spirit. This fact has led the Sri Lankan theologian, D.T. Niles, to observe that 'it is not just coincidence that there is a revival of the healing ministry of the church at the same time as there is the swelling of the Ecumenical Movement'.[18] It is in the context of ecclesial life that the Spirit exercises his ministry and distributes the gifts 'for the common good' (1 Cor. 12.7). Prayer for healing of the body, mind and spirit must be a regular part of the Pentecostal church's *liturgical* life. As James has taught us, the sick are to be prayed for and anointed with oil by the *elders* of the church. This has, for the most part, been preserved in the Eastern Church where the anointing with oil for healing was regularly practised. In fact, all believers received this sacrament once a year on the Friday before Palm Sunday.[19] As a healing and reconciling community the church can then extend its healing ministry to the larger world. In this connection Pentecostals must seriously rethink the popular practice of relying on a few gifted healing evangelists for the well-being of the church. One must question the usual method of trying to start a revival by inviting some well-known speaker with some supernatural gift to his or her credit, usually an independent preacher who takes pride in having no church affiliation. Such an approach is completely contrary to the work of the Spirit in the church. It implies that the church needs some external human agent to carry on its work. Whereas to believe in the Spirit-filled church means that the *charismata* operate freely within the life of the church, especially in the eucharistic event when the action of the Spirit is particularized. In short, the holy communion should be the best occasion for prayers of reconciliation and healing to take place.

It is also in recognition of the all-embracing healing work of the Spirit in the eucharistic event that Christian tradition concludes the celebration with the 'sending forth' (*missio*: the Mass)[20] in the power of the Spirit to offer healing and reconciliation to the world. We are fed and renewed in order to offer up our lives as living sacrifices to God to be used as he pleases. In the Anglican *Book of Common Prayer* the communion ends with the congregation praying this prayer:

18. D.T. Niles, *That They May Have Life* (New York: Harper and Brothers, 1951), p. 78.

19. See Stanley Burgess, 'Implications of Eastern Christian Pneumatology', in Jongeneel (ed.), *Experiences of the Spirit*, pp. 23-34 (30).

20. The Mass properly understood has nothing to do with the Catholic doctrine of transubstantiation, as commonly thought.

> Almighty God, we thank you for feeding us with the body and blood of
> your Son Jesus Christ. Through him we offer you our souls and bodies to
> be a living sacrifice. *Send us out* in the power of your Spirit to live and
> work to your praise and glory. Amen.

Eucharistic worship does not end in cosy fellowship, but in costly
mission into the world. The early Methodists captured this truth by
including a collection for the poor at the end of the communion service.

A Truth-Traditioning Community

Third, the action of the Spirit not only constitutes the church dynamically, it also makes the church the place where truth exists dynamically.
This means that connection between Christ the Truth, the Head of the
church, and the tradition of the church is far more profound than is
usually acknowledged in Protestantism. Christ who is the truth is not
just an individual, historical person, but is also the truth in relation to
the church as his Body. The church is therefore an extension of Christ
the truth.[21] The on-going traditioning in the church of Christ the truth is
made possible by the action of the Spirit. The dynamic relationship
between Christ and the church through the Spirit is seldom explicitly
acknowledged by Protestants. Pentecostals who have a far more
dynamic view of the Spirit's work in the church than their Protestant
counterparts *could* develop a closer relationship between Truth and
tradition. This is already seen in their understanding of the 'Spirit-
Word'. Steven Land observes that for Pentecostals the relationship
between Spirit and Word 'is based on that of the Spirit to Christ. Even
as the Spirit formed Christ in Mary, so the Spirit uses Scripture to form
Christ in believers and vice versa'.[22] The Spirit's work in the believers
is on-going and is not confined to just illuminating the Scriptures,
although what the Spirit says is always based on the truth of Scripture.
But the possibility of evolving a dynamic tradition is hampered by their
individualistic conception of the Pentecost event: Spirit-Word becomes
a *rhema*-word given to an individual resulting in a tendency towards
illuminism. The more 'orthodox' Pentecostals try to correct this danger
by a wooden doctrine of Scripture inherited from evangelicalism in
which illumination refers solely to the Spirit's work of applying the
Scripture to personal life. This 'safe' approach that limits the normative
traditioning of truth to the first century—the result of Pentecostal-evan-

---

21. Zizioulas, *Being as Communion*, pp. 110-14.
22. See Land, *Pentecostal Spirituality*, pp. 100-101.

gelical collaboration—is well illustrated in a contemporary gospel song:

> The Father gave the Son
> The Son gave the Spirit
> The Spirit gives us life
> So we can give the gift of love.
> And the gift goes on
> And the gift goes on
> And the gift goes on...[23]

The first three lines implicitly recognize the normative First Tradition. But then, the gift of the Son through the Spirit is individualized and dehistoricized, for the song goes on to say: 'God gave *each of us* a present [Christ] on that [Christmas] night so long ago...'[24] The gift that goes on is not the extension of the gift of Christ in the church, but simply a *pattern* of our giving of love to others.

A more adequate approach would be to locate the Spirit-Word within the ecclesial community and the eucharistic event to avoid illuminism and retain the dynamism of the Word. Only within their ecclesial location can Spirit and Word retain their dynamism and continuity. Christ as the truth in the church is realized in the eucharist where he is sacramentally present. Christ the truth is made present in the church by the action of the Spirit in the preaching of the Word and in the sacrament. This is not just a truth of history, subject to its relativities, but, because it is by the action of the Spirit, the truth of history (the gospel story) comes to us vertically and drives us forward into the future. John Zizioulas has expressed this thought most succinctly:

> [H]istory understood in the light of eucharistic experience is not the same as history as normally understood; it is conditioned by the *anamnetic* and *epicletic* character of the eucharist which, out of distance and decay, transfigures time into communion and life. Thus history ceases to be a succession of events moving from past to present linearly, but acquires the dimension of the future, which is also a vertical dimension transforming history into charismatic-pentecostal events. Within history thus pictured, truth does not come to us solely by way of delegation (Christ—the apostles—the bishops, in a linear development). It comes as a pentecostal event which takes linear history up into a charismatic present-moment.[25]

23. 'The Gift Goes On'. Words and Music by Ron Harris and Claire Cloninger. Copyright 1983 Ron Harris Music, used by permission.
24. Emphasis mine.
25. Zizioulas, *Being as Communion*, pp. 115-16.

Zizioulas's description of truth is significant for Pentecostals in at least two ways. First, it confirms the Pentecostal's insistence that truth is supernatural because of what the Spirit has done. Without this supernatural dimension the truth is in constant danger of being relativized. This was perhaps why the early Pentecostals were more fearful of the liberals than the fundamentalists. The liberals had de-supernaturalized truth and this would have completely undermined the fundamental structure of Pentecostal experience. Pentecostals, however, have not been as emphatic on the historical dimension of truth. Their strong sense of the Spirit's action has tended to lead them towards an 'over-supernaturalized' concept of truth. Here is where Zizioulas's concept of truth could again help the Pentecostal. The fact that the Spirit 'transfigures' history, turning it into a charismatic-pentecostal event means that history is important, otherwise there would be nothing to transfigure. History is the avenue by which the Pentecostal event takes place. It is through the ordinary elements of bread and wine that a new dimension of reality opens up by the Spirit's action. The Pentecostal event cannot be divorced from history, or there would be no historical continuity of the vertical event. Herein lies the Achilles' heel of Pentecostalism: by freeing the Pentecostal event from its historical moorings, it has considerably weakened its capacity for traditioning. If truth can come directly from the Spirit, what need is there to check it against the historical Christian tradition? The way for Pentecostals to overcome this weakness is by locating their experience in the ecclesial life, especially in the context of eucharistic worship where the ordinary things are 'transfigured'. Pentecostals would do well to appropriate the rich pneumatological resources in the Orthodox theology of the eucharist. If there is a sense in which the Spirit is especially present in the eucharist, could it not become the focal point of Pentecostal worship? Could it not be the occasion for prayer for a fresh in-filling of the Spirit for physical, emotional and spiritual healing?

Eschatology and the Church

The action of the Spirit in the church as a 'vertical' or 'pentecostal-charismatic' event raises the question of its relation to the past, present and future of history. The precise relation between the vertical and the historical must now be considered. Theologically, the issue could be seen as the relationship between pneumatology and eschatology.

The Spirit is the distinguishing sign of the 'last days' (Acts 2). The coming of the Spirit turns linear history into a present event. The Spirit unites the past and future in the present. This is seen repeatedly in Scripture where the Spirit is understood as the foretaste, the pledge or firstfruits of the new creation (Rom. 8.23). The Spirit coming from beyond history creates the church, or, we might say, the 'corporate personality' of Christ and points the church in the direction of the future, the beyond. To quote again from Zizioulas:

> The Spirit is the *beyond* of history, and when he acts in history he does so in order to bring into history the last days, the eschaton. Hence the first fundamental particularity of Pneumatology is its eschatological character.[26]

The presence of the Spirit in the church makes the church's existence to be essentially an eschatological existence in which the 'not yet' has in a sense 'already come'. Steven Land has well summed up the significance of this eschatological tension for Pentecostals:

> Pentecostals who are moved deeply and powerfully by the Spirit will laugh and cry, dance and wait in stillness. In the Spirit they 'already' participate in the marriage supper but also live in the 'not yet' of a lost world... [T]he Spirit acts as a kind of 'time machine' via the Word, enabling the believer to travel backward and forward in salvation and to imaginatively participate in the events that have been and are yet to be.[27]

The understanding of the church as the eschatological community constituted by the Spirit is extremely crucial for Pentecostal spirituality. First, the nature of the church's existence is basically characterized by its orientation to the future and the beyond. It is not merely a historical future but a future beyond history. This point is especially highlighted by Zizioulas and is something Pentecostals would find congenial to their own eschatological vision. It was such a vision that led early Pentecostals to be filled with such a 'passion for the kingdom' that everything else was made subservient to it. Christ as the coming king was not just one item in the five-fold gospel; it was, as Land has pointed out, the truth that gave shape to the five-fold gospel. Some Pentecostals might have over stressed the 'not yet' aspect of eschatology so much so that the 'imminence' of Christ's return tended to create a crisis mindset. While this apocalyptic vision has sometimes driven some to noble acts of service, it has unfortunately also resulted in disastrous ventures.

26. Zizioulas, *Being as Communion*, p. 130 (italics original).
27. Land, *Pentecostal Spirituality*, p. 98.

Second, the Spirit reminds us of the 'not yet', and at the same time he is the firstfruits of the new creation. We do have a foretaste of the future kingdom in this life—but only a foretaste. The powers of the age to come are already in some measure present in signs and wonders—but only a measure. The tension between the 'has come' and the 'not yet' must be carefully maintained. If some of the Pentecostals in an earlier period had tended to become too preoccupied with the 'not yet' modern charismatics like the 'Third Wavers' are often guilty of overplaying the 'kingdom now' theology. To maintain a healthy tension between the 'has come' and the 'not yet' our pneumatology must be interpreted primarily in the context of biblical eschatology rather than apocalypticism. Historically apocalypticism has resulted in either the abandonment of history or the adoption of false millennarian hopes. Biblical eschatology, by contrast, links the present and the future by the Spirit as the firstfruits of the new creation. It is as the firstfruits that we can begin to understand the Spirit's intercessory work in the church such as in Rom. 8.26. The 'unutterable groanings' of the Spirit in the believers is not primarily concerned with our personal intimacy with God but with the Spirit's work of identifying believers with the groanings of a broken world—a world that awaits the liberation of the children of God. The Spirit who inspires hope and points us to the 'beyond' of history does so without abandoning history but leads us *through* history to feel the birth pangs of the new age which in fact has already begun when the Spirit inaugurated the 'last days'. True Spirit-inspired prayer, far from privatizing our spiritual experience, should lead us to a deeper solidarity with the nonhuman creation. Real union with God by the Spirit cannot be too far removed from solidarity with God's world. The Spirit who drives us forward to a hope beyond history also drives us back into history, challenging us to take our historical existence with utmost seriousness. Pentecostals need to recover this dimension of glossolalic prayer; otherwise glossolalia can all too easily be reduced to privatized engagement with God and pious longing for a pie in the sky.

Third, the Spirit's relation to history brings out another important dimension of pneumatology: not only is the church Spirit-filled, but the church is also the special place where the Spirit is present on earth. We do not deny that the Spirit is present in creation and in the historical process, but the Spirit is present in the church in a way that he is not present in the world. In other words, it is not only true to say that the

Spirit constitutes the church giving the church its unique identity as a Spirit-filled body, but it is also true that the church thus constituted gives to the Spirit his distinctive character as the church-located and church-shaped Spirit. The latter concept could properly be called an ecclesiological pneumatology.[28] The Spirit's relationship to history is explicitly in and through the church. Pentecostals must continue to affirm this aspect of pneumatology especially against a growing tendency to 'free' the Spirit from his ecclesial location and release him into the world as Moltmann and the liberation theologians have done.[29] This tendency to universalize the Spirit's presence is often motivated by concerns for inter-religious dialogue and the status of non-Christian religions. An example can be seen in Gavin D'Costa, an inclusivist in the Rahnerian tradition, whose trinitarian approach to the issues involves reconceptualizing the role of the Spirit in universalistic terms: 'Pneumatology allows the particularity of Christ to be related to the universal activity of God in the history of humankind.'[30] But the scriptural account of the role and identity of the Spirit does not allow for *that* sort of universalization of pneumatology. As Kevin Vanhoozer has pointed out, 'the Spirit is the deputy of Christ rather than…an independent itinerant evangelist'.[31]

What is perhaps surprising is Hollenweger's call for greater openness to the concept of *Creator Spiritus* as the way forward to a more devel-

---

28. I am using ecclesiological pneumatology here to distinguish it from ecclesial pneumatology used earlier to refer to the corporate nature of Spirit-baptism in contradistinction to the filling of individuals. The distinction is necessary in view of the fact that while the doctrine of ecclesial Spirit-baptism is readily acknowledged by all, the concept of a special, restricted presence of the Spirit in the church has been questioned by some modern theologians. See n. 29 below.

29. Jürgen Moltmann, *The Spirit of Life: A Universal Affirmation* (Minneapolis: Fortress Press, 1992), pp. 8-10. The concept of the cosmic Spirit is pervasive in liberation theology. E.g. José Comblin, 'The Holy Spirit', in Jon Sobrino and Ignacio Ellacuría (eds.), *Systematic Theology: Perspectives from Liberation Theology* (London: SCM Press, 1996), pp. 146-64. Comblin speaks of the need to follow the 'signs' or ' "tracks" left by the Spirit' in liberation movements (p. 155).

30. Gavin D'Costa, 'Christ, the Trinity and Religious Plurality', in Gavin D'Costa (ed.), *Christian Uniqueness Reconsidered* (Maryknoll, NY: Orbis Books, 1990), p. 19.

31. Kevin Vanhoozer, 'Does the Trinity Belong in a Theology of Religions? On Angling in the Rubicon and the "Identity" of God', in *idem* (ed.), *The Trinity in a Pluralistic Age* (Grand Rapids: Eerdmans, 1997), pp. 41-71 (66).

oped Pentecostal pneumatology.[32] The one great difficulty with this concept is that we cannot adequately safeguard the Holy Spirit's identity unless the Spirit is understood in the context of an explicit trinitarian relationship. That means postulating special revelation and ecclesiological pneumatology, without which how can we tell apart the work of the Spirit of God from that of a shaman or a Taoist medium? How can we tell that an attractive liberation movement is a sign of the Spirit and not merely impelled by human ideology? The fact that so many liberation movements in history that were confidently hailed as signs of the Spirit turned out later to be just as oppressive and constrictive as the systems they replaced shows that discerning the Spirit in the world is not as easy as it is often made out to be. The reason is that the Spirit is not explicitly revealed in the world as he is in the church. What we would like to believe is the sign of God's Spirit often betrays a preference of one human ideology over another. Moltmann's 'cosmic Spirit', upon close scrutiny, turns out to be just a religious version of Western liberal egalitarianism which owes more to the Enlightenment than to Christianity.[33] Hollenweger, of course, recognizes the danger,[34] but I'm not as confident as he that this is really the way forward. Even if we could come to some decision that the spirit of the shaman belongs not to the prince of this world but 'to the good but confused order of creation, to the realm of the Creator Spiritus',[35] the question still remains: what does this do for the life and mission of the church? The issue is similar to the concept of the 'cosmic Christ' used by some Asian theologians like Stanley Samartha and Raimundo Pannikar to argue for the continuity between Christianity and other faiths as seen in their common concern for freedom, justice and human dignity, or their common affirmation of a mystery that undergirds all of life.[36] One

---

32. Walter Hollenweger, 'Priorities in Pentecostal Research: Historiography, Missiology, Hermeneutics and Pneumatology', in Jongeneel (ed.), *Experiences of the Spirit*, pp. 16-17.

33. See Arne Rasmusson, *The Church as Polis: From Political Theology to Theological Politics as Exemplified by Jürgen Moltmann and Stanley Hauerwas* (Notre Dame, IN: University of Notre Dame Press, 1995), pp. 248-302, esp. 290-94.

34. Hollenweger, 'Priorities in Pentecostal Research', pp. 17-18.

35. Hollenweger, 'Priorities in Pentecostal Research', p. 17.

36. Stanley J. Samartha, 'The Unbound Christ: Toward a Christology in India Today', in Douglas Elwood (ed.), *What Asian Christians are Thinking* (Manila: New Day Publishers, 1976), pp. 221-39; Raimundo Pannikar, *The Unknown Christ of Hinduism* (Maryknoll, NY: Orbis Books, rev. edn, 1981).

could, if one looks hard enough, always find some kind of common Christ-principle at work in other faiths, but that does not change the fact that it is interpreted within a belief system which is essentially non-Christian. What we have noted in Asia is that wherever the concept of the cosmic Christ is taken seriously, it has resulted in the blurring of distinction between church and world and a weakening of the church's proclamation of the gospel. A similar, if not more serious, consequence follows from the concept of *Creator Spiritus* except that instead of finding a common Christ-principle undergirding all faiths, one discovers a common Spirit-principle like artistic inspiration or spirit manifestations. The Christian tradition, however, has for the most part understood the goodness in creation as belonging not to the cosmic Christ or *Creator Spiritus* but to the *vestigia dei* (literally, the footprints of God).[37] On that understanding it has understood all that is true and good in any religion and culture as *praeparatio evangelii*. To see them as the manifestation of the Spirit assumes the presence of the new creation apart from the proclamation of the gospel. This goes against the consistent testimony of Scripture regarding the identity of the Spirit. As C.F.D. Moule has noted, 'Spirit is confined to the Church and the "new creation". Christ, as God's Wisdom and Word, has cosmic functions, but not the Spirit'.[38] The *revealed* identity of the Spirit is always the Spirit of the church and of the new creation. Any attempt to reinterpret his basic role is a gross distortion of pneumatology and trinitarian theology, and consequently misrepresents the nature and mission of the

---

37. E.g. Bonaventure, *Itinerarium Mentis ad Deum* 1.2, 11, etc. John Calvin uses *divinitatis sensum* (sense of divinity) and *semen religionis* (seed of religion) for the same thing (*Institutes of the Christian Religion* 1.3.1, 1.4.1). If anything, there is more biblical basis for the cosmic Christ (e.g. Col.) than for the cosmic Spirit. In the traditional understanding of creation, the Son is the link between the Trinity and creation. According to Bonaventure, the Son who is eternally generated out of the Father's fullness contains the archetypes of creation. The creatures could, therefore, be called the *vestigia Dei* in that they reflect the archetypes in the Son. Bonaventure uses this doctrine in developing the practice of meditation on the creatures, which constitutes the first two of six steps towards union with God. See 'Introduction', *Bonaventure* (trans. and intro. Ewert Cousins; Classics of Western Spirituality; New York: Paulist Press, 1978), pp. 25-27.

38. See C.F.D. Moule, *The Holy Spirit* (Grand Rapids: Eerdmans, 1978), p. 20. Cf. Tom Smail: 'When the New Testament refers to creation it does so not in relation to the Spirit but in relation to the Son, the Word by whom all things were made' (*The Giving Gift*, p. 168).

church. When Paul and Silas were at Philippi, they were met by a for-tune-teller who proclaimed, 'These men are servants of the Most High God, who are telling you the way to be saved' (Acts 16.17). Here might be a case for seeing the *Creator Spiritus* at work. After all, wasn't the fortune-teller clearly endorsing the ministry of the servants of God? But for Paul and Silas the occasion did not call for a discernment of the Spirit's work in other religions; it called for exorcism.

We are not saying that there is no place for the concept of *Creator Spiritus*, but its usage must be carefully circumscribed. The concept signifies God's dynamic relation to the cosmos which lays the founda-tion for sacramental theology: creation is an avenue of grace (cf. Ps. 19.1). But creation is not an independent means of grace, but requires interpretation from within the faith-community, the locus of special revelation, if it is to make any true sense.[39] In short, the concept of *Creator Spiritus* must be kept strictly within the boundaries of revealed knowledge; only then can it be used to clarify the relationship between Creator and creation.[40]

The Nicene Creed has wisely enjoined us to glorify the Holy Spirit 'together with the Father and the Son' and this must be the way in which the work of the Spirit is understood and discerned. As I have already noted, the canonical Scripture has little to say about the cosmic Spirit, although this idea is prominent in inter-testamental literature.[41] In Scripture the Spirit's relation to the world is primarily seen at the beginning and at the end: at creation (Gen. 1.2) and at the eschato-logical new creation (Rev. 22.17).[42] The reason is probably because it is

39. Joseph Ratzinger, *Principles of Catholic Theology: Building Stones for a Fundamental Theology* (San Francisco: Ignatius Press, 1987), p. 29. According to Colin Gunton, this is what a doctrine of revelation is meant to convey: it 'tells us that we cannot discover certain things unless we are taught them' ('The Trinity, Natural Theology, and a Theology of Nature', in Vanhoozer (ed.), *The Trinity in a Pluralistic Age*, pp. 88-103 (100).

40. God's relation to history is a little more complex in that it involves the question of the relationship between divine action and the action of free agents. It is not always possible to determine whether or to what extent a historical movement is a sign of God's working in history. Whatever that is true in the movement is better understood in terms of the *vestigia dei* than in terms of the *Creator Spiritus*.

41. See Moule, *The Holy Spirit*, pp. 7-21.

42. Some believe that the Spirit in the new creation is pictured in Rev. 22.1-5 as the river of life-giving water flowing from the throne of God and of the Lamb (cf. Isa. 44.3; Jn 7.38-39). If this is so, the Spirit is still viewed within the trinitarian

only before the Fall and after the restoration of the creation that the Spirit could be unmistakably revealed in creation. Whereas in a fallen creation the Spirit—'the person without a face'—could easily be confused with other spirits, as the pervasiveness of animism in many cultures shows—unless his identity is linked to the Father and the Son.[43]

If we accept the need for an ecclesiological pneumatology, then we also need to rethink the nature of the church's role in the world. Much of the modern discussion on the need for the church to be engaged with the world is based on the implicit belief of a *common* Spirit in the church and in the world. For example, as already mentioned, the liberation theologian will see certain liberating movements as signs of the Spirit of God at work. The role of the church, then, is to discern the presence of the Spirit in the socio-political structures and cooperate with the Spirit in advancing the kingdom of God in these structures. But an ecclesiological pneumatology will seek to engage the world in a different way. The church cannot influence the world by manipulating its power structures. In the missiological context, this manipulation has taken on the form of establishing a 'neutral' ground from which the universal truth-claims of Christianity could be commended to the world.[44] But as Mark Heim has pointed out, there is no neutral ground for sharing the Christian faith with the non-Christian. Its justification can only be sought from within the Christian belief system itself.[45] The church can only commend the gospel to the world by its own consistent character and proclamation. This is the only theologically coherent missionary strategy, as Lesslie Newbigin has persuasively argued.[46]

relationship. See Montague, *The Holy Spirit*, pp. 330-32.

43. Smail is even more cautious with regard to the Beginning and End: 'What...the New Testament approach is saying is that the work of the Spirit at the origin of things, like the work of the Spirit at the ultimate end of things, cannot be understood directly in and for itself but only in relation to Christ the incarnate Word who is the power and presence of God right in the midst of things' (*The Giving Gift*, p. 169).

44. The attempt of John Hick to develop a global theology based on a 'neutral' concept for ultimate reality, 'the Real', comes most readily to mind. The same presupposition is also at work behind Rahner's 'anonymous Christianity'. See John Hick, *An Interpretation of Religion* (New York: Yale University Press, 1989) and Rahner, 'Christianity and the Non-Christian Religions', pp. 115-34.

45. S. Mark Heim, *Salvations: Truth and Difference in Religion* (Maryknoll, NY: Orbis Books, 1995), esp. pp. 129-157.

46. Lesslie Newbigin, *The Gospel in a Pluralist Society* (Grand Rapids: Eerd-

This is also what the 'theological politics' of Stanley Hauerwas is seeking to do, and in recent years it is gaining an increasing number of influential supporters.[47] The church cannot influence the world simply by *doing* the right things; it must first be a 'community of character' and as such *be* a source of change in the world. The church believes in its ability to change the world simply by *being* the church because it sees itself as the community of Christ indwelled by the life-giving Spirit.

The Pentecostal Reality and Everyday Life

The Pentecostal ecclesial vision, with its ecclesiological pneumatology, raises another question of practical importance: How does the Pentecostal reality with its emphasis on extraordinariness in its ecclesial life defined by relationship to the Trinity, relate to the ordinary world of carrying out a vocation, raising a family, living the everyday life as a Christian? The question is important because Pentecostals have often been accused of being 'out of this world' or worse 'out of their minds' when it comes to mundane matters. To a certain extent this charge has some validity in so far as Pentecostals are too carried away by their apocalyptic vision. If this vision is not balanced by a nuanced biblical eschatology which maintains the tension between the 'has come' and 'not yet', a crisis mentality could set in. The Pentecostal way of life embodies the spirit of risk-taking and adventure, but the line between adventure and reckless venture is a thin one. The history of Pentecostalism could furnish us with many ready examples of people who had crossed the line.

Jean-Jacques Suurmond in his theology of play has provided a helpful way of finding a place for Pentecostal extraordinariness in the midst of ordinary life.[48] Building on the classic study of Johan Huizinga, Suurmond understands the charismatic experience as having the same logical function as play. Play is an occasion when people freely choose

mans, 1989), pp. 222-33.

47. For example, the various contributors to the collection of essays in Carl E. Braaten and Robert W. Jenson (eds.), *The Two Cities of God* (Grand Rapids: Eerdmans, 1997), esp. Robert W. Jenson, 'The Church's Responsibility for the World', pp. 1-10.

48. Jean-Jacques Suurmond, *Word and Spirit at Play: Towards a Charismatic Theology* (Grand Rapids: Eerdmans, 1994).

to suspend the ordinary course of life to enter into a world of free and spontaneous relationships. Some of Huizinga's observations about the nature of play are extremely pertinent to the Pentecostal reality.

> ...we might call [play] a free activity standing quite consciously outside 'ordinary' life as being 'not serious', but at the same time absorbing the player intensely and utterly. It is an activity connected with no material interest, and no profit can be gained by it. It proceeds within its own proper boundaries of time and space according to fixed rules and in an orderly manner. It promotes the formation of social groupings which tend to surround themselves with secrecy and to stress their difference from the common world by disguise of other means.[49]

According to Huizinga, the main characteristics of play are freedom and 'not "ordinary"'.[50] There is also the element of 'repetition and alternation'. The world of play, within the limit of time that the play is on, is a 'real' and 'perfect' world.

> Inside the play-ground an absolute and peculiar order reigns. Here we come across another, very positive feature of play: it creates order, *is* order. Into an imperfect world and into the confusion of life it brings a temporary, a limited perfection.[51]

We encounter in play the paradox of freedom and order. Play is freely embraced, yet within the world of play itself there is supreme order: the 'rules' of the game are sacrosanct. Further, in play we create a world which temporarily abolishes the ordinary world. Within the world of play, new understandings of life are discovered, new relationships are forged. We return from the world of play better able to deal with the challenges of 'ordinary' living.

Pentecostal worship has all the characteristic features of play, with the potential to forge a coherent and effective traditioning community. The Pentecostal community enters into 'free worship', and yet within that freedom and spontaneity there are certain game rules to make the freedom of play possible. These rules, however, are freely embraced. According to Suurmond, Pentecostal worship is characterized by the freedom of play between Word (the structure) and Spirit (freedom). It has its own implicit liturgy. But order must not become legalistic—

49. Johan Huizinga, *Homo Ludens: A Study of the Play Element in Culture* (Boston: Beacon Press, 1955 [1950]), p. 13.
50. Huizinga, *Homo Ludens*, p. 8.
51. Huizinga, *Homo Ludens*, p. 10.

which it can, when we are not critical towards it. This is why the uncritical use of unwritten rituals can be a great hindrance to true Pentecostal spontaneity, whereas if a traditional order is used critically it can be a powerful occasion to experience the freedom of Pentecostal 'play' or celebration.[52] Robert Webber has in fact shown that it is possible for traditional worship forms to be vitalized by a liberating Pentecostal celebration.[53]

Pentecostal worship, however, has not always realized this communal play and hence the potential for traditioning in worship. It is often hampered by a preoccupation with individualistic concerns. This is reflected in the overwhelming number of charismatic songs which focus on the big 'I'. Worship becomes the occasion to seek good feelings, and where the role of the worship leader is to create the right mood. Communal worship has been turned into 'a thousand individual experiences of worship'.[54]

Huizinga has also noted the 'uselessness' of play, that is, it is an end in itself. It serves no pragmatic purposes. Worship is similar: 'Only in the useless play of celebration is life taken seriously as a true gift of God.'[55] This truth has an important bearing on modern Pentecostal worship. There is a tendency in our culture-bound churches to find a pragmatic reason for worshipping God. Increasingly, we hear things like: praising God will bring down the presence of God. Cf. the popular charismatic chorus: 'And as we worship, build your throne...' We fast and pray in order to get the 'anointing' (Benny Hinn). Such a view of worship is diametrically opposed to the nature of worship: the end of worship is the worship of God, nothing more or less. But when worship is made into some purpose-driven activity, it is no longer worship. The name of it is magic, the manipulation of divine power for our own ends. This is why 'power healing' and 'power evangelism' where the focus is on power, are extremely dangerous, as seen in the work of Charles Kraft. Kraft's missionary strategy requires discovering the spiritual laws governing the spiritual world, especially the demonic world and using those laws against the powers of darkness.[56] This is no longer

52. Suurmond, *Word and Spirit*, p. 88.

53. Robert E. Webber, *The Worship Phenomenon* (Nashville, TN: Abbot Martyn, 1994).

54. Fee, *The First Epistle to the Corinthians*, p. 667.

55. Suurmond, *Word and Spirit*, p. 88.

56. See the article of Kraft in Edward Rommen (ed.), *Spiritual Power and*

gospel but spiritual power play; and power play is play that will destroy all plays. The end is spiritual dictatorship, where the one who wields spiritual power commands absolute obedience. This is a problem to which the Pentecostal-charismatic movement is more particularly prone precisely because it seeks more consciously to relate to the powerful workings of God.

Understanding Pentecostal worship as play helps us to relate better to ordinary life. The value of play is that it takes up a part of time; that is to say, there is always a beginning and end of play. But that part of time makes a difference to the rest of time. Life cannot be all play; neither can life be lived meaningfully without play. The Pentecostal reality *as* play, therefore, finds its own proper place in the less extraordinary way of living the Christian life. Without it, Christian life is manageable, but a lot more drab; with it, life takes on a depth and abundance that it is meant to have. And yet, like play, the Pentecostal reality cannot properly function apart from the larger context of the 'ordinary' Christian life. This is why it must always be interpreted within the larger Christian spiritual tradition where the ordinary and extraordinary, the predictable and unpredictable are woven together to form a coherent and rich tapestry of life with God the Father, in Christ through the Spirit. This brief study hopes to provide some pointers on how that could be done and some reasons why it must be done if Pentecostalism is to recover its original vision in the twenty-first century.

Missions: Raising the Issues (Pasadena, CA: William Carey Library, 1995) and my book review of *Spiritual Power and Missions* in *Dharma Deepika* 2.2 (Dec. 1996), pp. 96-98. For a sustained critique of the spiritualism in Kraft and Wagner, see Chuck Lowe, *Territorial Spirits and World Evangelization* (Mentor: OMF, 1998).

BIBLIOGRAPHY

Anon, *The Philokalia* (4 vols.; trans. G.E.H. Palmer, Philip Sherrard, Kallistos Ware; London: Faber and Faber, 1979-1995).

—*The Way of a Pilgrim and The Pilgrim Continues His Way* (trans. Helen Bacovcin; New York: Image Books, 1978).

Anselm, *Prayers and Meditations of St Anselm with the Proslogion* (trans. Benedicta Ward; London: Penguin Books, 1973).

Appasamy, A.J., *Sundar Singh: A Biography* (Madras: The Christian Literature Society, 1990 [1958]).

Aquinas, Thomas, *Summa Theologiae* (60 vols; New York: Blackfriars, 1964–).

Atkinson, William, 'Pentecostal Responses to Dunn's Baptism in the Holy Spirit: Luke–Acts', *Journal of Pentecostal Theology* 6 (1995), pp. 87-131.

Baer, Richard A., Jr. 'Quaker Silence, Catholic Liturgy, and Pentecostal Glossolalia—Some Functional Similarities', in Spittler (ed.), *Perspectives on the New Pentecostalism*, pp. 152-54.

Balthasar, Hans Urs von, *Mysterium Paschale* (trans. Aidan Nichols; Grand Rapids: Eerdmans, 1993).

Barth, Karl, *Church Dogmatics* (4 vols.; trans. G.W. Bromiley; Edinburgh: T. and T. Clark, 1975).

Bloesch, Donald, *A Theology of Word and Spirit* (Downers Grove, IL: InterVarsity Press, 1992).

Blumhofer, Edith L., 'Purity and Preparation: A Study in the Pentecostal Perfectionist Heritage', in Stanley M. Burgess (ed.), *Reaching Beyond: Chapters in the History of Perfectionism* (Peabody, MA: Hendricksen Press, 1986), pp. 270-79.

Bonaventure, *Bonaventure: The Soul's Journey into God, The Tree of Life and the Life of St Francis* (trans. and intro. Ewert Cousins; Classics of Western Spirituality; New York: Paulist Press, 1978).

Bonfoeffer, D., *Letters and Papers from Prison* (ed. Eberhard Bethge; trans. Reginald H. Fuler; New York: Macmillan, 1966).

Braaten, Carl E., and Robert W. Jenson (eds.), *The Two Cities of God* (Grand Rapids: Eerdmans, 1997).

Braaten, Carl E., *Mother Church: Ecclesiology and Ecumenism* (Minneapolis: Fortress Press, 1998).

Bridges-Johns, Cheryl, *Pentecostal Formation: A Pedagogy among the Oppressed* (Sheffield: Sheffield Academic Press, 1993).

Burgess, Stanley M., *The Holy Spirit: Ancient Christian Tradition* (Peabody, MA: Hendriksen Press, 1984).

—'Implications of Eastern Christian Pneumatology', in Jongeneel (ed.), *Experiences of the Spirit*, pp. 23-34.

Cassian, John, *The Conferences* (trans. Boniface Ramsey O.P.; New York: Paulist Press, 1997).

Chan, Simon, 'Sharing the Trinitarian Life', in Thomas F. Best and Günther Gassmann (eds.), *On the Way to Fuller Koinonia* (Geneva: WCC Publications, 1994), pp. 83-90.

—*Spiritual Theology: A Systematic Study of the Christian Life* (Downers Grove, IL: InterVarsity Press, 1998).

Chesterton, G.K., *Orthodoxy* (Garden City, NY: Image Books, 1959).

Childs, Brevard S., *Biblical Theology of the Old and New Testaments* (Minneapolis, MN: Fortress Press, 1993).

Christensen, Michael J., *C.S. Lewis on Scripture* (London: Hodder & Stoughton, 1979).

Clark, Mathew S., *et al.*, *What is Distinctive About Pentecostal Theology?* (Pretoria: University of South Africa, 1989).

Comblin, José, 'The Holy Spirit', in Sobrino and Ellacuría (eds.), *Systematic Theology*, pp. 146-64.

Congar, Ives M.J., *I Believe in the Holy Spirit* (3 vols.; trans. David Smith; New York: Seabury Press, 1983).

Culligan, Kevin G. O.C.D. (ed.), *Spiritual Direction: Contemporary Readings* (Locus Valley, NY: Living Flame, 1983).

Cutsinger, James S. (ed.), *Reclaiming the Great Tradition* (Downers Grove, IL: InterVarsity Press, 1997).

D'Costa, Gavin (ed.), *Christian Uniqueness Reconsidered* (Maryknoll, NY: Orbis Books, 1990).

Dempster, Murray, 'The Church's Moral Witness: A Study of Glossolalia in Luke's Theology of Acts', *Paraclete* 23.1 (Winter 1989), pp. 1-7.

Doctrine Commission, *We Believe in the Holy Spirit: A Report by the Doctrine Commission of the General Synod of the Church of England* (London: Church House Publishing, 1993).

Dorman, David A., 'The Purpose of Empowerment in the Christian Life', *Pneuma* 7.2 (Fall 1985), pp. 147-65.

Downey, Michael (ed.), *The Dictionary of Catholic Spirituality* (Bangalore: Theological Publications of India, 1995).

Edwards, Jonathan, *The Religious Affections* (Edinburgh: Banner of Truth Trust, 1986 [1746]).

Edwards, Tildern, *Spiritual Friend: Reclaiming the Gift of Spiritual Direction* (New York: Paulist Press, 1980).

Elwood, Douglas (ed.), *What Asian Christians are Thinking* (Manila: New Day Publishers, 1976).

Erikson, Erik, *Identity and the Life Cycle: Selected Papers* (New York: International Universities Press, 1959).

—*The Life Cycle Completed* (New York: Norton, 1982).

Farley, Edward, *Theologia: The Fragmentation and Unity of Theological Education* (Philadelphia: Fortress Press, 1983).

Faupel, D. William, 'Glossolalia as Foreign Language: An Investigation of the Early Twentieth-Century Pentecostal Claim', *Wesleyan Theological Journal* 31.1 (Spring 1996), pp. 95-109.

—*The Everlasting Gospel* (Sheffield: Sheffield Academic Press, 1996).

—'Whither Pentecostalism?' *Pneuma* 15.1 (Spring 1993), pp. 9-27.

Fee, Gordon, 'Baptism in the Holy Spirit: The Issue of Separability and Subsequence', *Pneuma* 7.2 (Fall 1985), pp. 87-100.

—*God's Empowering Presence: The Holy Spirit in the Letters of Paul* (Peabody, MA: Hendricksen Press, 1994).

—*The First Epistle to the Corinthians* (Grand Rapids: Eerdmans, 1987).

Fowl, Stephen E., *Engaging Scripture: A Model for Theological Interpretation* (Oxford: Basil Blackwell, 1998).

Fowler, James, *Stages of Faith: The Psychology of Human Development and the Quest for Meaning* (San Francisco: Harper & Row, 1981).

Gelpi, Donald L. S.J., 'Breath-Baptism in the Synoptics', in Robeck, Jr (ed.), *Charismatic Experiences*, pp. 15-43.

Groeschel, Benedict J., *Spiritual Passages: The Psychology of Spiritual Development* (New York: Crossroad, 1983).

Gunkel, Hermann, *The Influence of the Holy Spirit* (trans. Roy A. Harrisville and Philip A. Quanbeck II; Philadelphia: Fortress Press, 1979 [1888]).

Gunton, Colin, 'The Trinity, Natural Theology, and a Theology of Nature', in Vanhoozer (ed.), *The Trinity in a Pluralistic Age*, pp. 88-103.

Hauerwas, Stanley, *A Community of Character: Toward a Constructive Christian Social Ethic* (Notre Dame: University of Notre Dame Press, 1981).

Hausherr, Irénée, *The Name of Jesus: The Names of Jesus Used by Early Christians. The Development of the 'Jesus Prayer'* (trans. Charles Cummings; Kalamazoo, MI: Cistercian Publications, 1978).

Heiler, Friedrich, *The Gospel of Sadhu Sundar Singh* (trans. Olive Wyon; New Delhi: ISPCK, 1989).

Heim, S. Mark, *Salvations: Truth and Difference in Religion* (Maryknoll, NY: Orbis Books, 1995).

Hick, John, *An Interpretation of Religion* (New York: Yale University Press, 1989).

Hocken, Peter, 'Pentecostals on Paper II: Baptism in the Spirit and Speaking in Tongues', *The Clergy Review* 60 (1975), pp. 161-83.

—'The Meaning and Purpose of "Baptism in the Spirit"', *Pneuma* 7.2 (Fall 1985), pp. 125-34.

—'The Significance and Potential of Pentecostalism', in *New Heaven? New Earth?* (Springfield, IL: Templegate Publishers, 1976), pp. 15-67.

Hollenweger, Walter, 'The Critical Tradition of Pentecostalism', *Journal of Pentecostal Theology* 1 (1992), pp. 7-17.

—*The Pentecostals* (Peabody, MA: Hendricksen Press, 1988).

Hui, Archie, 'The Spirit of Prophecy and Pauline Pneumatology', *Tyndale Bulletin* 50.1 (1999), pp. 93-115.

Huizinga, Johan, *Homo Ludens: A Study of the Play Element in Culture* (Boston: Beacon Press, 1955 [1950]).

Hurtado, Larry W., 'Normal, but Not a Norm: "Initial Evidence" and the New Testament', in McGee (ed.), *Initial Evidence*, pp. 189-201.

Jones, Cheslyn, Geoffrey Wainwright and Edward S.J. Yarnold (eds.), *The Study of Spirituality* (London: SPCK, 1986).

Jongeneel, Jan A.B. (ed.), *Experiences of the Spirit* (Frankfurt Am Main: Peter Lang, 1991).

Kildahl, John, *The Psychology of Speaking in Tongues* (New York: Harper & Row, 1972).

Kohlberg, Lawrence, *The Psychology of Moral Development: The Nature and Validity of Moral Stages* (San Francisco: Harper & Row, 1984).

Land, Steven J., *Pentecostal Spirituality: A Passion for the Kingdom* (Sheffield: Sheffield Academic Press, 1993).

Leclercq, Jean, *The Love of Learning and the Desire for God* (New York: Fordham University Press, 1985).

Lederle, Henry, *Treasures Old and New* (Peabody, MA: Hendrickson Press, 1988).

—'Initial Evidence and the Charismatic Movement: An Ecumenical Appraisal', in McGee (ed.), *Initial Evidence*, pp. 131-41.

Lewis, C.S., *Surprised by Joy* (London: Geoffrey Bles, 1955).

Lindbeck, George A., *The Nature of Doctrine: Religion and Theology in a Postliberal Age* (Philadelphia: Westminster Press, 1984).

Lloyd-Jones, Martin, *Joy Unspeakable: Baptism with the Holy Spirit* (Eastbourne, E. Sussex: Kingsway Publications, 1984).

Lovelace, Richard, 'Baptism in the Holy Spirit and the Evangelical Tradition', *Pneuma* 7.2 (Fall 1985), pp. 101-24.

Lowe, Chuck, *Territorial Spirits and World Evangelization* (Mentor: OMF, 1998).

Lubac, Henri de, *The Motherhood of the Church* (trans. Sr. Sergia Englund, O.C.D.; San Francisco: Ignatius Press, 1971).

Macchia, Frank D., 'Groans Too Deep for Words: Towards a Theology of Tongues as Initial Evidence', *Asian Journal of Pentecostal Studies* 1.2 (1998), pp. 149-73.

—'Sighs Too Deep For Words: Toward a Theology of Glossolalia', *Journal of Pentecostal Theology* 1 (1992), pp. 47-73.

—'Tongues as a Sign: Towards a Sacramental Understanding of Pentecostal Experience', *Pneuma* 15.1 (Spring 1993), pp. 61-76.

MacIntyre, Alasdair, *After Virtue: A Study in Moral Theory* (Notre Dame, IN: University of Notre Dame Press, 1981).

McConnell, D.R., *A Different Gospel: A Historical and Biblical Analysis of the Modern Faith Movement* (Peabody, MA: Hendrickson Press, 1988).

McDonnell, Kilian, and George T. Montague, *Christian Initiation and Baptism in the Holy Spirit: Evidence from the First Eight Centuries* (Collegeville, MN: Liturgical Press, 1991).

McDonnell, Kilian, 'The Function of Tongues in Pentecostalism', *One in Christ* 19.4 (1983), pp. 332-54.

McGee, Gary G. (ed.), *Initial Evidence: Historical and Biblical Perspectives on the Pentecostal Doctrine of Spirit Baptism* (Peabody, MA: Hendricksen Press, 1991).

McGinn, Bernard, *The Presence of God: A History of Western Mysticism* (3 vols.; London: SCM Press, 1991-1998).

McGrath, Alister E., *The Genesis of Doctrine* (Oxford: Basil Blackwell, 1990).

Menzies, Robert and Wonsuk Ma (eds.), *Pentecostalism in Context* (Sheffield: Sheffield Academic Press, 1997).

Menzies, Robert P., *Empowered for Witness: The Spirit in Luke–Acts* (Sheffield: Sheffield Academic Press, 1994).

—'Evidential Tongues: An Essay on Theological Method', *Asian Journal of Pentecostal Studies* 1.2 (July 1998), pp. 111-23.

—'Paul and the Universality of Tongues: A Response to Max Turner', *Asian Journal of Pentecostal Studies* 2.2 (July 1999), pp. 283-95.

—*The Development of Early Christian Pneumatology with Special Reference to Luke–Acts* (Sheffield: JSOT Press, 1991).

Michaels, Ramsey J., 'Evidences of the Spirit, or the Spirit as Evidence? Some Non-Pentecostal Reflections', in McGee (ed.), *Initial Evidence*, pp. 202-207.

Mills, Watson E. (ed.), *Speaking in Tongues* (Grand Rapids: Eerdmans, 1988).

Moltmann, Jürgen, *The Spirit of Life: A Universal Affirmation* (Minneapolis: Fortress Press, 1992).

Montague, George T., *The Holy Spirit: Growth of a Biblical Tradition* (Peabody, MA: Hendrickson Press, 1976).

Moule, C.F.D., *The Holy Spirit* (Grand Rapids: Eerdmans, 1978).

Murphy, Nancey, Brad J. Kallenberg and Mark Thiessen Nation (eds.), *Virtues and Practices in the Christian Tradition* (Harrisburg, PA: Trinity Press International, 1997).

Nelson, Douglas J., 'For Such a Time as This: The Story of Bishop William J. Seymour and the Azusa Street Mission' (PhD dissertation, University of Birmingham, 1981).

Newbigin, Lesslie, *The Gospel in a Pluralist Society* (Grand Rapids: Eerdmans, 1989).

Niles, D.T., *That They May Have Life* (New York: Harper and Brothers, 1951).

—*The Message and its Messengers* (Nashville, TN: Abingdon Press, 1966).

O'Connor, Edward, 'The Hidden Roots of the Charismatic Renewal in the Catholic Church', in Vinson Synan (ed.), *Aspects of Pentecostal-Charismatic Origins* (Plainfields, NJ: Logos International, 1975), pp. 169-91.

O'Keefe, Mark, 'The Three Ways', *Studies in Formative Spirituality* 13.1 (February 1992), pp. 73-83.

Ong, Walter, *The Presence of The Word: Some Prolegoumena for Cultural and Religious History* (New Haven: Yale University Press, 1967).

Pannikar, Raimundo, *The Unknown Christ of Hinduism* (Maryknoll, NY: Orbis Books, rev. edn, 1981).

Penny, John, *The Missionary Emphasis of Lukan Pneumatology* (Sheffield: Sheffield Academic Press, 1997).

Pinnock, Clark H., *Flame of Love: A Theology of the Holy Spirit* (Downers Grove, IL: InterVarsity Press, 1996).

Polanyi, Michael, *The Tacit Dimension* (Gloucester, MA: Peter Smith, 1983).

Polkinghorne, John, *Serious Talk: Science and Religion in Dialogue* (London: SCM Press, 1996).

Poloma, Margaret, *The Assemblies of God at the Crossroads: Charisma and Institutional Dilemmas* (Knoxville, TN: University of Tennessee Press, 1988).

Price, Robert M., 'Confirmation and Charisma', *St Luke's Journal of Theology* 23.3 (June 1990), pp. 173-83.

Puddefoot, John C., 'Indwelling: Formal and Non-Formal Elements in Faith and Life', in Torrance (ed.), *Belief in Science*, pp. 28-48.

Rahner, Karl, 'Christianity and the Non-Christian Religions', in *Theological Investigations*, V (trans. Karl H. Kruger; London: Darton, Longman & Todd, 1966), pp. 115-34.

—'Priest and Poet', in *Theological Investigations*, III (trans.; 22 vols.; London: Darton, Longman & Todd, 1967), pp. 294-317.

Rasmusson, Arne, *The Church as Polis: From Political Theology to Theological Politics as Exemplified by Jürgen Moltmann and Stanley Hauerwas* (Notre Dame, IN: University of Notre Dame Press, 1995).

Ratzinger, Joseph, *Principles of Catholic Theology: Building Stones for a Fundamental Theology* (San Francisco: Ignatius Press, 1987).

Robeck, Jr. Cecil M. (ed.), *Charismatic Experiences in History* (Peabody, MA: Hendricksen Press, 1985).

—'Taking Stock of Pentecostalism: The Personal Reflections of a Retiring Editor', *Pneuma* 15.1 (Spring 1993), pp. 35-60.

Rommen, Edward (ed.), *Spiritual Power and Missions: Raising the Issues* (Pasadena, CA: William Carey Library, 1995).

Samartha, Stanley J., 'The Unbound Christ: Toward a Christology in India Today', in Elwood (ed.), *What Asian Christians are Thinking*, pp. 221-39.

Scalise, Charles J., *From Scripture to Theology: A Canonical Journey into Hermeneutics* (Downers Grove, IL: InterVarsity Press, 1996).

Schreiter, Robert J., *Constructing Local Theologies* (London: SCM Press, 1985).

Shelton, James B., *Mighty in Word and Deed: The Role of the Holy Spirit in Luke–Acts* (Peabody, MA: Hendrickson, 1991).

Sheppard, Gerald, 'Pentecostalism and the Hermeneutics of Dispensationalism: The Anatomy of an Uneasy Relationship', *Pneuma* 6.2 (Fall 1984), pp. 5-34.

Shuman, Joel, 'Toward a Cultural-Linguistic Account of the Pentecostal Doctrine of the Baptism of the Holy Spirit', *Pneuma* 19.2 (Fall 1997), pp. 207-23.

Smail, Tom, *The Giving Gift: The Holy Spirit in Person* (London: Hodder & Stoughton, 1988).

Sobrino, Jon, and Ignacio Ellacuría (eds.), *Systematic Theology: Perspectives from Liberation Theology* (London: SCM Press, 1996).

Spittler, Russell P. (ed.), *Perspectives on the New Pentecostalism* (Grand Rapids: Baker Book House, 1976).

Steinmetz, David C., 'The Superiority of Pre-Critical Exegesis', in Stephen E. Fowl (ed.), *The Theological Interpretation of Scripture* (Oxford: Basil Blackwell, 1997), pp. 26-38.

Stronstad, Roger, *The Charismatic Theology of St Luke* (Peabody, MA: Hendricksen Press, 1984).

Suenens, Léon Joseph, *A New Pentecost?* (trans. Francis Martin; New York: Seabury Press, 1975).

Sullivan, Francis A., *Charisms and Charismatic Renewal: A Biblical and Theological Study* (Ann Arbor, MI: Servant Books, 1982).

Suurmond, Jean-Jacques, 'The Meaning and Purpose of Spirit-Baptism and the Charisms', in Jongeneel (ed.), *Experiences of the Spirit*, pp. 35-62.

—*Word and Spirit at Play: Towards a Charismatic Theology* (Grand Rapids: Eerdmans, 1994).

Synan, Vinson (ed.), *Aspects of Pentecostal-Charismatic Origins* (Plainfields, NJ: Logos International, 1975).

Tan, May Ling, 'A Response to Frank Macchia's "Groans Too Deep for Words: Towards A Theology of Tongues as Initial Evidence"', *Asian Journal of Pentecostal Studies* 1.2 (July 1998), pp. 175-83.

Teresa of Avila, *The Collected Works of St Teresa of Avila* (2 vols.; trans. Kieran Kavanaugh and Otilio Rogriguez; Washington, DC: ICS Publications, 1980).

Thomas, John Christopher, 'Max Turner's *The Holy Spirit and Spiritual Gifts: Then and Now* (Carlisle: Paternoster Press, 1996): An Appreciation and Critique', *Journal of Pentecostal Theology* 12 (1998), pp. 3-22.

—'Pentecostal Theology in the Twenty-First Century', *Pneuma* 20.1 (Spring 1998), pp. 3-19.

Torrance, Thomas F., *Theological Science* (London: Oxford University Press, 1969).

Torrance, Thomas F. (ed.), *Belief in Science and in Christian Life* (Edinburgh: Hansel Press, 1980).

Tugwell, Simon, *Did you Receive the Spirit?* (London: Darton, Longman & Todd, 1972).

—The Speech-Giving Spirit: A Dialogue with Tongues', in *New Heavens? New Earth?* (Springfield, IL: Templegate Publishers, 1976), pp. 119-59.

Turner, Max, *The Holy Spirit and Spiritual Gifts in the New Testament Church and Today* (Peabody, MA: Hendrickson, rev. edn, 1998).

—'Tongues: An Experience for All in the Pauline Churches?' *Asian Journal of Pentecostal Studies* 1.2 (July 1998), pp. 231-53.

Underhill, Evelyn, *Worship* (Guildford, Surrey: Eagle, 1991 [1936]).

Vanhoozer, Kevin J. (ed.), *The Trinity in a Pluralistic Age* (Grand Rapids: Eerdmans, 1997).

Volf, Miroslav, *After our Likeness: The Church as the Image of the Trinity* (Grand Rapids: Eerdmans, 1998).

—*On Prayer* (London: SPCK, 1961).

—*The von Balthasar Reader* (eds. Medard Kehl and Werner Löser; trans. Robert J. Daly; New York: Crossroad, 1982).

Ward, Benedicta, trans., *Sayings of the Desert Fathers: The Alphabetical Collections* (Kalamazoo, MI: Cistercian Publications, 1975).

—*The Wisdom of the Desert Fathers: Apophthegmata Patrum* (Oxford: SLG Press, 1975).

Ward, Neville, *The Use of Praying* (London: Epworth Press, 1988 [1967]).

Ware, Kallistos, 'The Spiritual Director in Orthodox Christianity', in Culligan (ed.), *Spiritual Direction*, pp. 21-23.

Webber, Robert E., *The Worship Phenomenon* (Nashville, TN: Abbot Martyn, 1994).

Wesley, John, and Charles Wesley, *Hymns on the Lord's Supper* (Facsimile reprint; Madison, NJ: The Charles Wesley Society, 1995).

—'John and Charles Wesley: Selected Writings and Hymns', in Franking Whaling (ed.), *Classics of Western Spirituality* (New York: Paulist Press, 1981).

Wesley, John, *The Journal of the Rev. John Wesley, A.M.* (8 vols.; ed. Nehemiah Curnock; London: Charles H. Kelly, 1909-1916).

Williams, Rowan, *Teresa of Avila* (Harrisburg, PA: Moorehouse Publishing, 1991).

Yong, Amos, ' "Tongues of Fire" in the Pentecostal Imagination: The Truth of Glossolalia in the Light of R.C. Neville's Theory of Religious Symbolism', *Journal of Pentecostal Theology* 12 (1998), pp. 39-65.

Zizioulas, John D., *Being as Communion* (Crestwood, NY: St Vladimir's Seminary Press, 1993 [1985]).

INDEXES

INDEX OF REFERENCES